CUTTING-EDGE table saw tips & tricks

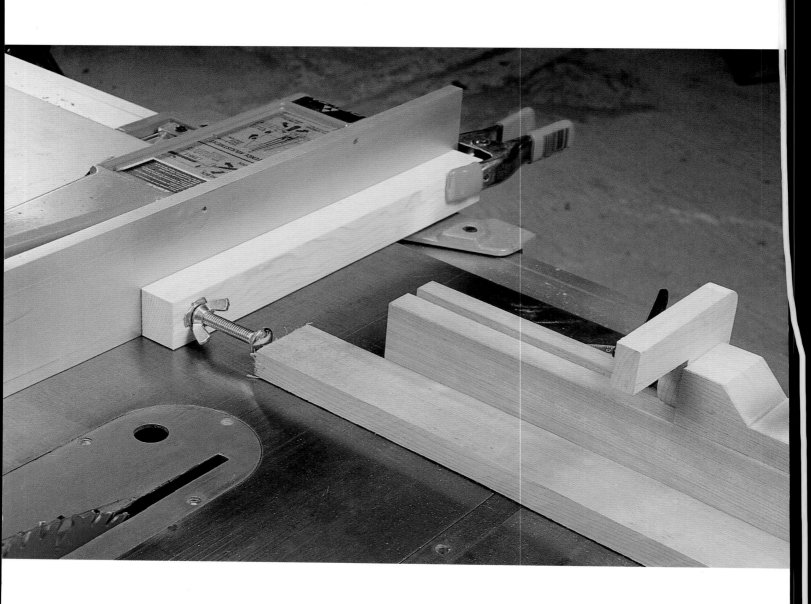

CUTTING-EDGE
table saw
tips & tricks

*How to get the most
out of your saw*

KENNETH BURTON

POPULAR
WOODWORKING
BOOKS

CINCINNATI, OHIO
www.popularwoodworking.com

Visit our Web site at www.popularwoodworking.com for information on more resources for woodworkers.

Other fine Popular Woodworking Books are available from your local bookstore or direct from the publisher.

07 06 05 04 03   5 4 3 2 1

Library of Congress Cataloging-in-Publication Data

Burton, Kenneth S.
   Cutting-edge table saw tips & tricks / by Kenneth Burton.-- 1st ed.
   p. cm.
   ISBN 1-55870-623-2
   1. Circular saws. 2. Woodwork. I. Title.
   TT186 .B85 2003
   684'.083--dc21
                              2002012894

Editor: Jim Stack
Associate Editor: Jennifer Ziegler
Designer: Brian Roeth
Layout Artist: Kathy Gardner
Project Opener Photos: Mitch Mandel
Step-by-step photos: Kenneth Burton
Technical Illustrations: Kenneth Burton & Jim Stack
Production coordinated by Mark Griffin

READ THIS IMPORTANT SAFETY NOTICE

To prevent accidents, keep safety in mind while you work. Use the safety guards installed on power equipment; they are for your protection. When working on power equipment, keep fingers away from saw blades, wear safety goggles to prevent injuries from flying wood chips and sawdust, wear headphones to protect your hearing, and consider installing a dust vacuum to reduce the amount of airborne sawdust in your woodshop. Don't wear loose clothing, such as neckties or shirts with loose sleeves, or jewelry, such as rings, necklaces or bracelets, when working on power equipment. Tie back long hair to prevent it from getting caught in your equipment. People who are sensitive to certain chemicals should check the chemical content of any product before using it. The authors and editors who compiled this book have tried to make the contents as accurate and correct as possible. Plans, illustrations, photographs and text have been carefully checked. All instructions, plans and projects should be carefully read, studied and understood before beginning construction. Due to the variability of local conditions, construction materials, skill levels, etc., neither the author nor Popular Woodworking Books assumes any responsibility for any accidents, injuries, damages or other losses incurred resulting from the material presented in this book. Prices listed for supplies and equipment were current at the time of publication and are subject to change. Glass shelving should have all edges polished and must be tempered. Untempered glass shelves may shatter and can cause serious bodily injury. Tempered shelves are very strong and if they break will just crumble, minimizing personal injury.

METRIC CONVERSION CHART

to convert	to	multiply by
Inches	Centimeters	2.54
Centimeters	Inches	0.4
Feet	Centimeters	30.5
Centimeters	Feet	0.03
Yards	Meters	0.9
Meters	Yards	1.1
Sq. Inches	Sq. Centimeters	6.45
Sq. Centimeters	Sq. Inches	0.16
Sq. Feet	Sq. Meters	0.09
Sq. Meters	Sq. Feet	10.8
Sq. Yards	Sq. Meters	0.8
Sq. Meters	Sq. Yards	1.2
Pounds	Kilograms	0.45
Kilograms	Pounds	2.2
Ounces	Grams	28.4
Grams	Ounces	0.035

For my wife Susan, who has put up with more than her share of sawdust and unfinished cabinets.

About the Author

Ken Burton has been working with wood professionally for the past 20 years and writing about it for the past 12. He holds an MFA degree from the School for American Crafts at the Rochester Institute of Technology.

Currently, Burton operates Windy Ridge Woodworks in New Tripoli, Pennsylvania, where he designs and builds studio furniture, custom cabinetry and teaches woodworking workshops. He also teaches at the Yestermorrow School in Warren, Vermont.

During the school year, Burton is department leader for the MST program at Boyertown Area Senior High. MST is a unique program that combines the disciplines of math, science and technology.

Husband of Susan and father of Sarah, Burton has a to-do list about 4 miles long. You can contact him at ksburton@fast.net.

Acknowledgements

A special thanks to all those who helped make this book a reality. To Susan, who put up with me while I was writing, and to Sarah, who graciously waited until later to play Neopets on our computer. To Jared Haas (Mr. Hands in many of the photos), who stood by patiently for many hours waiting for me to get the lighting right. To Jeff Day, my best friend and partner in many ventures, and Paul Anthony, a good friend and conspirator, who both generously gave of their time and expertise to help out. To my father, Ken Burton, Sr., who loaned me his table saw, and Bill Ash, who lent me his.

Thanks, also, to the many people who sent various tools and toys for me to try out, including Nita Miller at Biesemeyer Manufacturing, Charles Bazikian at Forrest Manufacturing, Karen Powers at Freud Tools, Norm Hubert at LRH Enterprises, Don Guillard at Woodcraft Supply and Cliff Paddock at CMT USA, Inc.

And finally to the crew at Popular Woodworking Books, including my editor, Jim Stack, Jenny Ziegler, Brian Roeth and Mark Griffin: Thanks for taking on this project and turning out such a great-looking book.

table of contents

chapter one
essential
operations
page 10

chapter two
joinery
page 28

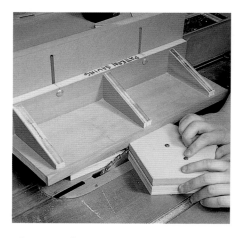

chapter three
shaping
page 62

chapter four
cutting sheet
stock
page 80

chapter five
tuning up your
saw
page 92

introduction

Cutting-Edge Table Saw Tips & Tricks grew out of a weekend class I run in my studio called Table Saw Trickery. The class is designed to present a sweeping overview of all the different tricks you can make your table saw do. It is intended for beginning and intermediate woodworkers who are looking to upgrade their skills and get more out of their saws. I cover everything from cutting wood to size efficiently and accurately, to shaping and precision joinery. This is a pretty tall order for a weekend; however, those who take the class tell me they really get a lot out of it. Over the past seven years, I have come to appreciate this type of quick, intensive learning as a way to help woodworking enthusiasts improve their skills without taking a big chunk of time out of anyone's schedule.

This book was written with the same mind-set. It is not especially long, but it is packed full of shop-tested techniques that cover the entire range of what a table saw can do. Not only will these techniques yield good results, but they will also help you accomplish these results efficiently and, most importantly, safely.

I encourage you to try these techniques in your own shop: Adapt them to your equipment and to your ways of working. If I've learned one thing about working with wood, it is that there are many ways to get the job done. During the classes I teach, I think I often learn just as much as my students because of all the questions that start out "Why can't you?"

After you finish reading all of the tips and tricks, you may want to start using them by building one of the projects from the back of the book. They were designed with a table saw in mind. The spice cabinet is the project we build in the class. Its construction is relatively straightforward, and it packs a lot of different techniques into a small package. It can be easily built in a weekend, and it will expand your appreciation of what you can accomplish with a table saw. Or try the tabletop valet with its drawers and moulded mirror frame to push your saw technique a little beyond the ordinary. And for a bit more of a challenge, tackle the demilune table. It features bentwood aprons and the tricky joinery that goes along with pieces that aren't straight.

Some things to be aware of: While a few simple jigs and fixtures are scattered throughout the book, I have never been one who builds really complicated jigs and fixtures. The few that show up are ones that I have found especially useful. Some, such as the box joint jig, give you the capacity to make a cut that you simply could not do any other way. Others, such as the tenoning jig or the crosscut extension fence, are so handy that they are really worth investing a little extra time and effort in.

Also, this book is not intended as a buying guide to saws and saw accessories. While I do make a few general suggestions, if you want more specific recommendations, get one of the woodworking magazines that publishes tool reviews, such as *Popular Woodworking*. They are in a much better position to publish up-to-date information about current models than I can offer in this book. As for accessories, I have included a few specialized items simply because of the added techniques they allow you to accomplish. The market certainly has a lot more goodies available. About the only advice I can offer is: Try to see the item in question in operation before you invest.

Finally, using a table saw is not without risks. The techniques I have included here are all safe and shop-tested. However, they are not foolproof. If something doesn't seem right to you, or makes you hesitate, don't do it. Consult with someone who is familiar with the technique or try to find some other way around it. Better yet, come take one of my classes; we welcome woodworkers of all experience levels.

I hope you enjoy the book and put it to good use.

Ken Burton
Windy Ridge Woodworks
2002

> "My table saw is something of a hybrid. The basic machine is a Powermatic model 66. To it I've added a Delta Unifence, a Biesemeyer splitter and an Excalibur blade cover. With all that, plus a few blades and other cutters, I can make dust with the best of them."

essential operations

AS YOU WILL SOON SEE, THE TABLE saw is an incredibly versatile machine. Joinery, shaped profiles, tapers and more are all within the tool's capabilities. At the root of all of these operations is the table saw's ability to cut a straight line. Being able to saw straight is what makes accurate woodworking possible. Cutting a board to an exact width (ripping) and cutting it to a precise length (crosscutting) are the two essential operations that come into play with almost every project. Before getting into these matters in more depth, let's look at the table saw itself and a few general guidelines about its operation.

■ *types of saws*

There are essentially four types of table saws, the size of which is determined by the largest-diameter blade the saw can handle. Portable saws are lightweight models that are easy to move from place to place. They are great for carpentry because they can be set up near wherever you are working. They are also good for woodworkers who don't have the space for a larger model. In exchange for portability, however, portable saws often have smaller motors and are limited in the size of pieces they can cut. Portables usually can spin either an 8"- or a 10"-diameter blade.

The next step up is a contractor's saw. This stationary saw sits on an open base. The motor generally hangs off the rear of the machine, and it takes a 10" blade. Contractor's saws usually have a bit more power and capacity than portable saws.

For more money, you can purchase a cabinet saw. Cabinet saws have an enclosed base with a motor that hangs below the blade/arbor assembly. The added weight of the base and lower center of gravity help cut down on vibration, which makes for a smoother cut. This is the type of saw many small professional shops use. It will probably have enough power and capacity to handle any job you throw at it. Sizes range from 10" through 16".

At the top of the heap are the European-style saws with a built-in sliding table. These are designed for serious production work and come equipped with an equally serious price tag.

If you are in the market for a saw, a myriad of choices is available. Which to choose depends a lot on the work you intend to do and the space you have available. Unless you are really cramped for space, or intend to move the saw around a lot, I recommend either a contractor's saw or a cabinet saw. If you work primarily in pine and only occasionally cut thick (2") hardwoods, a contractor's saw will be perfectly adequate. If, however, you work mainly in hardwood, you will quickly appreciate the added power a cabinet saw has to offer.

Make sure your electrical system can handle the load from the saw's motor. Most contractor's saws can be plugged into a standard 120-volt outlet. Cabinet saws, on the other hand, require more juice. These saws have a 3-horsepower motor, which requires a 220-volt line with a 30-amp fuse or circuit breaker.

Another thing to consider is the capacity of the saw's rip fence. For most work in solid wood, a fence with a maximum capacity of 24" is adequate. If you intend to cut a lot of sheet stock, however, you'll be happier if your fence reaches 48" or more away from the blade.

■ *saw blades*

You'll need at least one saw blade. Most saws come with some kind of blade, but chances are it won't be a particularly good one. While you can still purchase steel blades, most woodworkers find that the durability and accuracy of carbide-tipped blades make them worth the added expense. If you buy just a single blade, try to find a combination blade. These blades are designed to do a good job of both ripping and crosscutting. I leave my combination blade on the saw most of the time.

As you add blades to your collection, the next one to acquire is a rip blade (especially if your saw is on the underpowered side). A good, sharp rip blade can make a big difference in how easy it is to cut through hardwood stock such as oak or maple. Finally, add a precision crosscut blade for making exacting joinery cuts.

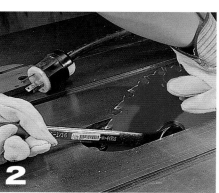

Rather than jamming a piece of wood against the blade (which can bend a tooth), the folks at Forrest recommend tightening the arbor nut by resting the wrench against the saw table and turning the blade by hand. Wear work gloves to protect your fingers and make sure the saw is unplugged.

For most general-purpose work, a quality combination blade such as Freud's LU84 or Forrest's Woodworker II will yield great results. When you're doing a lot of ripping, switch over to a rip blade such as Freud's LM72. The limited number of teeth means the blade requires less power to cut cleanly. For exacting crosscuts, a precision cutoff blade such as Freud's LU85 will produce a glasslike surface.

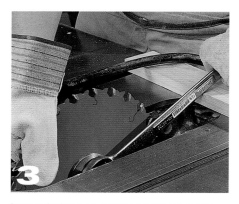

Loosen the blade by slipping the wrench on the arbor nut and rotating the blade until the wrench rests against the table at the back of the opening. Grasp the blade firmly and turn it backwards, freeing the nut. Again, wear gloves to protect your fingers. If the nut is particularly tight, place a scrap of wood across the opening and turn the blade so the wrench breaks the nut free.

Loosening and Tightening Blades

As I was researching blades for this book, I talked to Charles Bazikian at Forrest Manufacturing. As part of our discussion, he asked how I loosened and tightened the blades on my saw. When I told him I used a piece of wood to hold the blade in place while I worked the wrench, I could feel him cringe over the phone. He explained how Forrest had found that this technique (typical among many woodworkers) can bend a tooth on the blade – not much, but enough to affect the quality of the cut. As Forrest strives to produce blades that leave a glue-line-ready surface, a tooth bent even 0.002" to 0.003" leaves a surface that is rough enough to see and feel.

Note: My saw is equipped with a electronic brake, which cuts the speed of the blade when the power is turned off. I have discovered (the hard way) that if you do not adequately tighten a blade, the arbor nut will come loose when the brake kicks in. While this didn't cause an accident, it didn't do my blade any good either. The problem is worse with a dado head, I suspect, because the dado has a lot more mass than a blade. If your saw is equipped with a brake, be sure to tighten the arbor nut with a wrench. Bazikian's technique works on my saw, but I am sure to wear gloves so I can really get the nut tight.

■ **SAFETY FIRST**

Key Rules for Ripping

For safe, trouble-free rips, make sure:
- Your workpiece sits flat on the saw table.
- Your workpiece has a straight edge to run against the fence.
- You have installed a splitter on your saw.

Ripping

Ripping is cutting a piece of wood with the grain, or parallel to the direction in which the tree grew. You rip a board to straighten its edges and to make it the right width. Ripping is one of the two basic table saw operations; crosscutting (described later in this chapter) is the other. Most of the time, ripping involves cutting a piece that is at least as long as it is wide. If this is true, you can use the rip fence as a guide as you push the board through the cut. If the board is wider than it is long, use the miter gauge to guide the piece even though you are "ripping" it.

To make a rip cut, you need to set the rip fence at the necessary distance from the blade. For example, if you need a piece that is 6" wide, set the fence 6" away from the blade. As with all operations, the proof is then in the actual cut. If the dimension is really critical, start the cut, just nicking the end of the piece with the blade, then back the workpiece out and measure from the edge to the kerf to be sure the fence is set properly.

Kickback

Of all the operations done on the saw, ripping is potentially the most dangerous. The danger comes from a phenomenon called kickback. Kickback occurs when the blade throws your workpiece back at you. With even a modestly powered saw, this can happen with astonishing speed and force. Should kickback occur, your fingers can be pulled into the blade or a flying board can hit you.

Kickback can occur for two reasons: Either your workpiece comes away from the fence as you are guiding it through the cut, or the kerf (the space the blade produces as it cuts) may close and pinch the back side of the blade. The first situation is largely due to operator error. You need to be constantly aware of what is happening to your piece as you push it through the cut. The second situation can occur if you are cutting warped wood, or if the piece you are cutting warps as it is cut. With warped wood, the answer is straightforward: Don't cut it. Every piece you cut should sit flat on the saw table and should have a straight edge to run along the fence. To create a straight edge, use a jointer or see "Straight-Line Ripping" later in this chapter.

The truly scary situation is when you cut a board that warps as it passes by the blade. Every once in a while you may come up against a board that, for whatever reason (something about the way the tree grew, improper drying, etc.), bows and twists as it is cut. There can be no way of knowing this will happen until it is too late. So how do you deal with this possibility? The answer is to use a guard.

Guards

Table saw guards are, at best, something of a nuisance. However, they are critical to the safe operation of your saw. So, rather

The guard that came with my saw was cumbersome and involved loosening and tightening two bolts every time I installed or removed it. So while I was researching the material for this book, I looked into other options. I settled on the Biesemeyer splitter. Once the bracket is installed on the saw, the splitter itself can be set in place or removed in seconds by pulling on a knob, no other tools required. I really like this splitter, especially because I can use it in conjunction with my Excalibur blade cover, which includes a vacuum pickup for dust collection.

than storing yours on a shelf someplace, get to know how it works so you can use it effectively. To this end, here are a few things to recognize about saw guards.

First, not everything you do on the saw requires the guard. Second, the guard will actually be in the way for some operations and should be removed. Third, for some operations, such as ripping, a guard should *always* be used. Finally, you do not have to be stuck with the flimsy, ungainly guard that came with your saw. You can purchase a number of aftermarket guards, or you can make your own guard fairly easily. (See "Shop-Made Splitters" later in this chapter.)

Most stock guards consist of three parts: a blade cover, a splitter and one or two antikickback pawls. The cover keeps your fingers away from the blade, the splitter holds the kerf open and the pawls prevent the workpiece from being thrown back at the operator. These may all be incorporated into a single device, or they may be separate items. Of the three parts, the splitter (sometimes called a riving knife) is the most important and does the most to prevent kickback. Even if you use no other guard, you should not rip without a splitter in place.

No Tape Needed!

Many better-quality rip fences have an adjustable hairline pointer that you can set so it reliably indicates the distance between the fence and the blade. To set the pointer, use a tape to set the fence at some known distance from the blade, say 2". Test the setup, then set the pointer to match. Note: If you switch between a regular blade and a thin-kerf blade, you may have to reset the pointer accordingly.

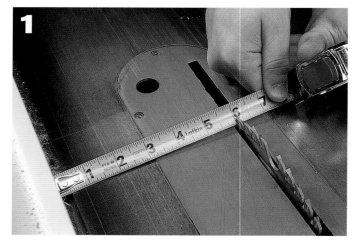

Measure to set the rip fence the specified distance from the blade. If your saw fence doesn't stay predictably parallel to the blade, measure twice — once near the front of the blade, and once near the rear. Add an extra $1/16$" to the cut if you want to joint away the saw marks later.

Stand to the left of the blade. Use your left hand to hold the workpiece against the fence in front of the blade. This hand should never move past the leading edge of the blade. Push the piece past the blade with your right hand.

■ SAFETY FIRST

Don't Let Go

Finish every cut before letting go. Even if you have some-one helping, be sure to push the workpiece all the way past the blade before letting go of it. The saw operator has far more control over the piece than does a helper, who would have to pull the piece clear of the blade.

Make sure the workpiece stays against the fence as you push it past the blade. If the piece is wide enough (3" or more, depending on your level of con-fidence), it is perfectly safe to push the piece all the way through the cut with your right hand.

For narrower cuts (less than 3"), use a push stick to push the piece the last few inches through the cut. Do not push on the offcut piece with your left hand; you can cause it to pinch the blade.

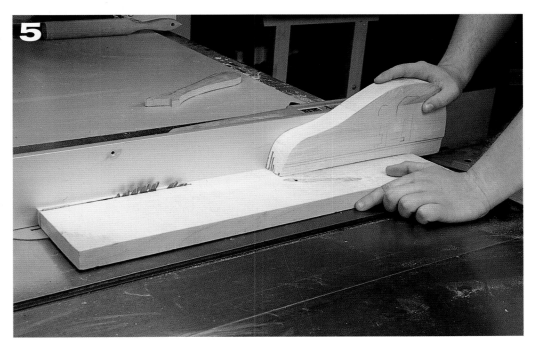

In my shop, push sticks are consum-able items. They quite often get cut when I am ripping narrow pieces. Just be sure to keep the push stick along the fence so it goes straight past the blade. In this operation, the push stick itself serves as a blade cover, and a shop-made splitter keeps the kerf open.

■ *shop-made splitters*

Despite the dangers, many saw owners relegate their saw guards to a dusty shelf or to the trash can, feeling the guards "get in the way," or "are more trouble than they are worth." In many cases, these feelings are well justified. The stock guards that come with many saws are often ill-conceived, clumsy affairs that are difficult to make behave properly. However, rather than doing without the benefits of a guard completely, there are two ways of making a splitter that will serve admirably. Both of these splitters are incorporated into shop-made throat plates. For details on making the plates, see "Making Throat Plates" in chapter five, "Tuning Up Your Saw."

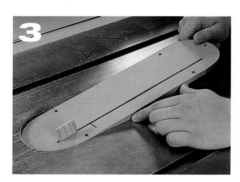

1 Make a throat plate and set it in place upside down in the saw table. Position the rip fence to hold the plate in place as you raise the blade to its highest setting. Lower the blade and flip the plate over. Raise the blade to its highest setting again. Mark the position of the back of the blade on the plate when the blade is at its highest setting.

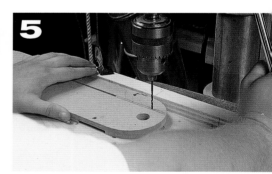

2 Cut a strip of hardwood to fit snugly in the slot cut in the plate. The piece should be about 1"-wide by 2"-long; its thickness will depend on the width of the kerf. Drill and counterbore holes in the edge of the plate. Fasten the splitter in place with round-head wood screws. (Flathead screws may split the plate if it is made of medium-density fiberboard.)

3 As a final step, chamfer the front edges of the splitter slightly with a file to make it easier to push your workpieces past. Set the throat plate aside for use when ripping.

4 An alternative approach is to use two cutoff steel drill bits as a splitter. After cutting the opening in the plate, use a pencil to carefully extend the lines made by the sides of the cut.

5 Drill two holes for the bits, carefully centering them between the lines. The holes should be about 1¼" apart and about 1" behind the blade opening. Use bits that are slightly smaller than the width of the blade kerf. For a ⅛" kerf, a No. 31 bit works well. Cut the bits short, then epoxy them in place.

■ push sticks

TOOL TALK

Push Sticks

Every shop I have ever worked in has had
its own push stick designs. Some of them I
have liked a lot, others not so much. All of
them, however, served to keep my fingers a
safe distance from the blade. The two designs shown here are those that I settled on
as my favorites. The one at the top is my
"standard issue," used for all general-purpose ripping. The one below is particularly
nice for narrow rips (under ¼" or so). As I
stated earlier, I view push sticks as a con-
sumable item, so I make three or four at a
time and toss them in the scrap bin when
they are no longer serviceable.

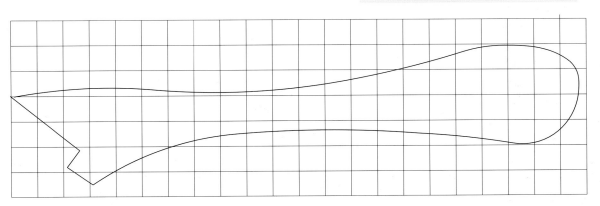

Make from 3/8" Stock   Each square represents 1/2"

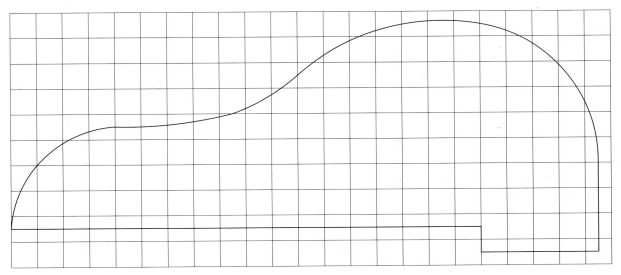

Make from 1 1/2" stock 2x6   Each square represents 1/2"

flush trimming

When I make bookshelves and other cabinetry, I often work with hardwood-veneered plywood. This material saves a lot of time and effort, but it usually requires its edges to be covered with some kind of edge-banding. I use strips of ¼"-thick solid hardwood for this purpose, cutting it slightly wider than the thickness of the plywood, and glue it in place. Cutting it slightly wide means I don't have to be as careful when I glue it in place. However, when the glue dries, I am faced with the job of trimming the edging flush with the face of the plywood. I have used a router to make these cuts, but have found that the small diameter of the router bit often causes the edging to splinter. So instead, I have come to rely on my table saw for this task. It is faster than the router and doesn't tend to chew up the edging.

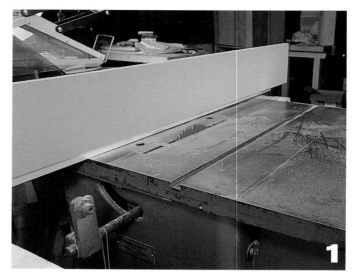

To set up for flush trimming, attach an auxiliary fence to your rip fence. I have drilled a couple of holes in my fence for such purposes. The auxiliary fence is simply a scrap of ¾" plywood about 8" × 30". Fasten it in place so it is about ¾" above the table.

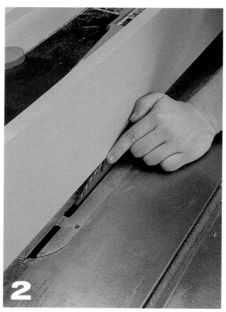

Raise the blade so it barely touches the underside of the auxiliary fence. Move the rip fence over so the auxiliary fence overhangs the blade ever so slightly. You can check this with your finger. Lock the fence in place.

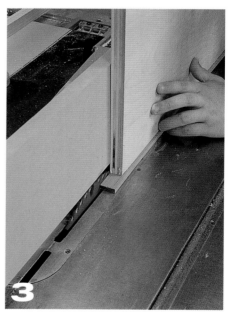

To make a cut, guide your workpiece on edge along the auxiliary fence. If you have to put edging on all four sides of a piece, you'll have to attach the edging in stages. Glue up two opposing sides, trim them, then glue up the two remaining sides.

■ *straight-line ripping*

Some large millwork shops and lumber-yards have a machine similar to a table saw called a straight-line rip saw. As the name implies, a straight-line rip saw cuts a straight edge on a piece of lumber without using any part of the workpiece as a reference. In contrast, you need to start with a straight edge on your workpiece to serve as a guide when you send it through a table saw.

In a large commercial setting, such a specialized piece of equipment can make sense; however, you have to run a lot of wood through it to justify both the cost and the space it takes up. For the occasional piece of wood you need to straighten out, you can adapt a table saw to achieve the same result. The key is to attach the board to a carrier that will serve as a straightedge.

I have seen a number of jigs people have devised for this purpose with adjustable clamping systems and whatnot. To my mind, however, unless you do this operation on almost a daily basis, these specialized jigs are overkill. For this type of operation I rely on a very simple system. I keep a length of 1×8 pine by my saw. (The current piece is about 60" long.) This serves as a carrier for the workpiece. To this piece, I screw pieces of 1×3 to locate the workpiece and to serve as attachment points for a pair of toggle clamps. The clamps hold the workpiece in place as I push the whole mess through the saw. The same carrier board also serves as my taper jig, which you will see later ("Cutting Tapers" in chapter three, "Shaping").

Start by determining where you want to cut the piece. Snap a chalk line to help you visualize the cut.

Position the workpiece on the carrier board so the chalk line aligns with the edge of the carrier. Place the 1×3 clamping blocks along the edge of the workpiece near either end and screw them to the carrier. Screw the clamps to the 1×3s and adjust them to hold the workpiece securely.

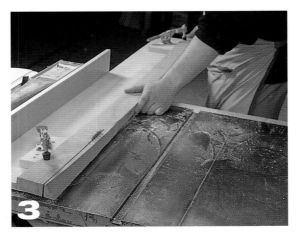

Set the distance from the blade to the rip fence to match the width of your carrier board. Run the carrier along with the attached workpiece through the saw, guiding the straight edge of the carrier against the fence. Be sure to use a splitter for safety.

▣ *crosscutting*

In addition to ripping, the other basic table saw operation is crosscutting, or cutting across the grain. To some people, crosscutting is a fairly generic term encompassing any cut across the grain, but to me it means making a 90° cut across the end of a board. You crosscut a board to cut it to length. A cut across a board at any other angle is a miter. (See "Cutting Miter Joints" in chapter two, "Joinery.")

For accurate crosscutting, you need a precise means of guiding your workpiece past the blade. Here, you have three options: a miter gauge, a crosscut sled and a sliding table. Each of these has advantages and disadvantages.

Most table saws come with two slots in its table and an accompanying miter gauge. Provided the saw is tuned up well and the miter gauge is properly adjusted, this setup will yield good results, especially with relatively short pieces. Its accuracy and efficiency can be improved by adding an auxiliary fence and a stop-block.

A crosscut sled is a shop-made jig that rides in the miter gauge slots. It carries the workpiece (rather than allowing it to slide along the saw table like a miter gauge does), so it is less prone to slippage than a miter gauge. A sled also makes it easier to control larger pieces as you crosscut them.

Similar to a sled is a sliding table. This accessory is either built into the saw or added on as an aftermarket accessory. With the best sliding tables, the entire saw table to the left of the blade moves. With add-on sliders, the movable table sits to

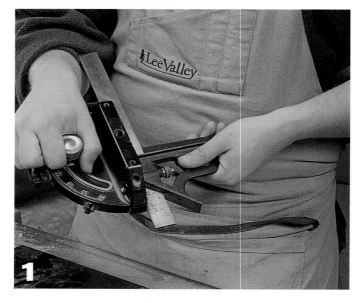

Set your miter gauge for a square cut by holding an accurate square along the bar and pivoting the head until it aligns with the square's blade.

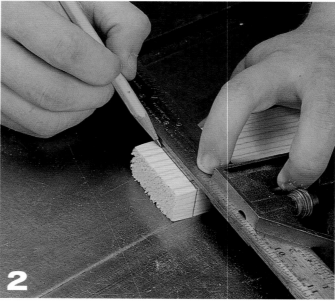

Lay out the cut across one face and one edge of your workpiece. If you are cutting the piece to length, cut one end square first, then measure from that end to mark the other cut.

the left of the saw's regular table. Sliding tables excel when cutting plywood and other sheet stock. They do, however, require a fair amount of space to the left of the saw and can be fussy to adjust.

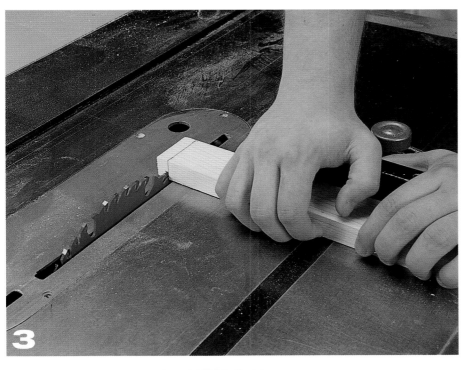

Slide the rip fence well out of the way. Squeeze the workpiece firmly against the face of the miter gauge and push it past the blade. For the most accurate cut, be sure some wood is on both sides of the blade. This balances the forces acting on the blade, keeping it from distorting.

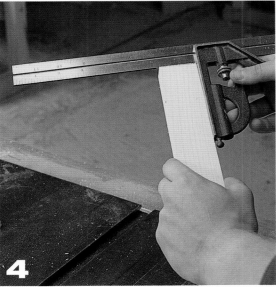

The true test of whether your miter gauge is properly adjusted is whether or not the cut is square. Before committing your good stock to a setup, make a test cut and check it with an accurate square.

Adding an extension fence (which can be as simple as a straight length of wood) to your miter gauge will greatly improve its accuracy and efficiency. By clamping a stop-block to the fence, you won't have to measure for multiple cuts after measuring the first piece. Even for a single cut, a stop-block will help keep the workpiece from shifting.

You can purchase a number of aftermarket miter gauges for your saw. These usually include an auxiliary fence along with a built-in stop. They also have a system for setting the gauge at many commonly used settings.

A step beyond an auxiliary fence, a sled provides a stable platform for crosscutting wide workpieces. You may want to make two sleds — a smallish one to accommodate pieces up to about 15" wide, and a big one for wider work.

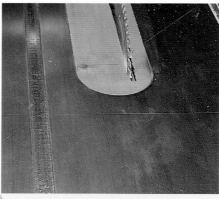

Scribed Settings

hot tip

For a quick reference, you can scribe a square line across the surface of your saw table. This will allow you to quickly set your miter gauge for square (or any other angle you care to scribe). To scribe these reference lines, carefully set your miter gauge to make a square cut and test it to be sure it is accurate. Hold the gauge in position slightly in front of the blade and scribe the table along the miter gauge's face with an awl.

Miter Gauge Extension Fence

While a straight length of scrap wood screwed to your miter gauge along with a small C-clamp or hand screw makes a perfectly serviceable auxiliary fence, the fence detailed here is much nicer. It features a built-in, adjustable stop that will swing out of the way and is constructed in such a way that it is practically warp-proof.

Make the fence from two pieces of 4/4 stock, preferably something with very straight grain that you have had in your shop for a while. (If you have to purchase wood to make the fence, allow it to adjust to your shop's atmosphere for several weeks before cutting it.) Cut the pieces to the profile as shown in the End View on the following page. Epoxy the pieces together (I used West System's basic epoxy) with an aluminum bar in the lower groove. Note that the bar does not run the whole length of the fence. Put a thin strip of plastic packing tape over the upper grooves to keep any epoxy from oozing out and making a mess.

Once the epoxy dries, carefully joint and plane the fence so it is absolutely straight and true. The embedded aluminum bar should help keep it that way. Cut a groove along the top of the fence, making the upper groove into a T-slot. Cut a tongue on the bottom of the mobile block to fit in this groove. Drill down through the mobile block for the locking stud.

Cut a piece of $1/8$" x 1" x $1^1/2$" band iron to serve as a lock nut. Drill and tap a hole in the band iron to receive the locking stud. Screw a threaded insert into the thick end of the mobile block for the ratchet arm that controls the stop. Cut and drill the stop as shown. Mount the fence to your miter gauge and you should be ready to go.

Note: The aluminum bar stops about 3" from the end of the fence. This gives you space to cut into the fence if need be. Should you accidentally cut into the aluminum, however, don't panic. Aluminum cuts quite well with carbide-tipped saw blades without damaging them.

By adding this shop-made extension fence to your miter gauge, you can get premium miter gauge performance at a rock-bottom price.

The aluminum bar running through the extension fence helps keep the fence from warping. While the bar is placed out of the way of the blade, it will not damage your blade if you should happen to cut through it.

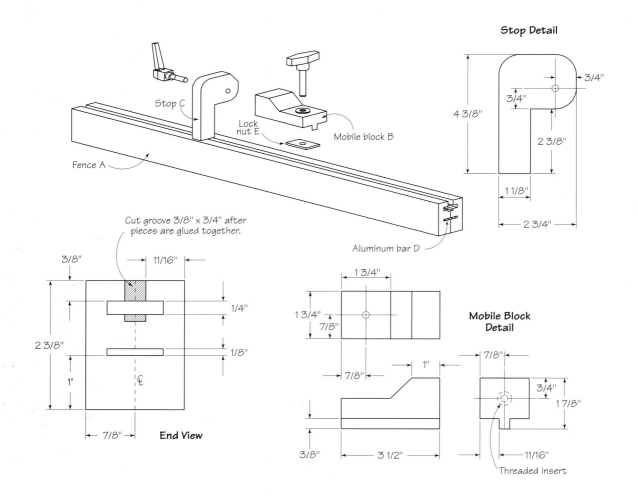

Stop Detail

Stop C

Lock nut E

Mobile block B

Fence A

Cut groove 3/8" x 3/4" after pieces are glued together.

Aluminum bar D

End View

Mobile Block Detail

Threaded insert

REFERENCE	QUANTITY	PART	STOCK	THICKNESS	WIDTH	LENGTH
A	2	fences	hard maple	$7/8$	$2^3/8$	27
B	1	mobile block	hard maple	$1^3/4$	$1^7/8$	$3^1/2$
C	1	stop	hard maple	$5/8$	$2^3/4$	$4^3/8$
D	1	aluminum bar	hard maple	$1/8$	1	24
E	1	lock nut	steel band	$1/8$	1	$1^1/2$

MATERIALS LIST inches

HARDWARE

T-knob
Woodcraft #27R16

Ratchet handle
Woodcraft #129132

Threaded insert to fit handle

REFERENCE	QUANTITY	PART	STOCK	THICKNESS	WIDTH	LENGTH
A	2	fences	hard maple	22	61	686
B	1	mobile block	hard maple	44	47	89
C	1	stop	hard maple	16	70	112
D	1	aluminum bar	hard maple	3	25	610
E	1	lock nut	steel band	3	25	38

MATERIALS LIST millimeters

HARDWARE

T-knob
Woodcraft #27R16

Ratchet handle
Woodcraft #129132

Threaded insert to fit handle

Fitting a Miter Gauge Bar to Its Slot

One of the critical factors in getting good results from a miter gauge is having the miter gauge bar fit well in its slot. This fit is actually something of a compromise. The bar can't be too tight, or the miter gauge will be difficult to move. But if the bar is too loose, the miter gauge won't provide consistent results. Too loose is usually the problem.

■ miter gauge

A quick way to make the miter gauge bar wider, and thus fit more snugly in its slot, is to dimple it periodically (every 2" to 3") along its length with a center punch.

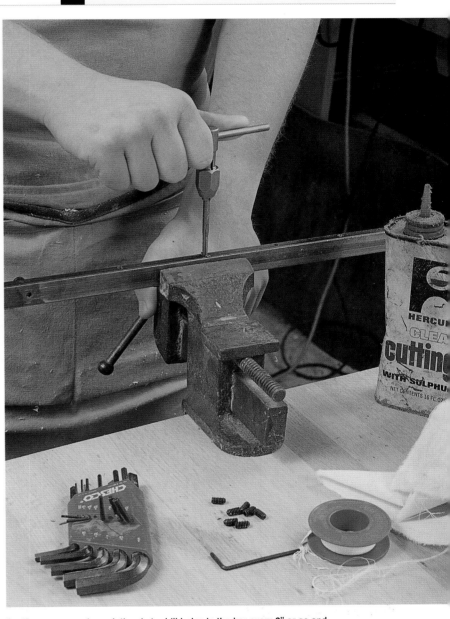

Another, more precise solution, is to drill holes in the bar every 2" or so and then to tap the holes and screw in No. 8 set screws. Wrap the set screws with Teflon plumber's tape or give them a squirt of Locktite (available at many auto-parts stores) to help them hold their adjustment. For No. 8 set screws, use a No. 29 drill bit and a tap to match the thread count.

making short crosscuts

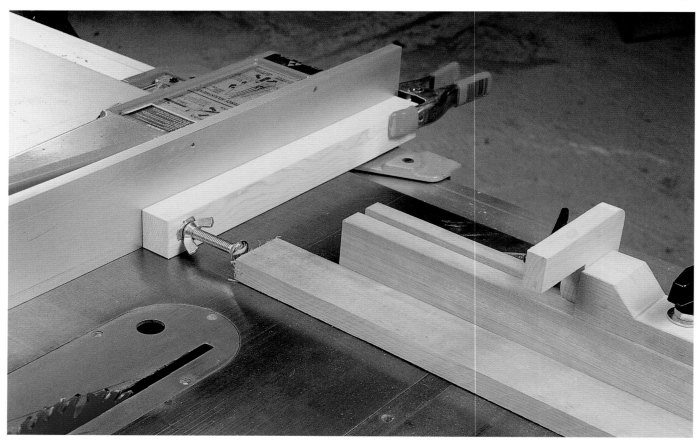

Many times, you have to make a series of short pieces — less than 5" or so long. With such short pieces, attaching a stop-block to the miter gauge fence, and then holding the pieces against it, puts your fingers dangerously close to the blade. Instead, you might be tempted to use the rip fence as a stop in conjunction with the miter gauge. This is a bad idea because as soon as you complete the cut, the cutoff is trapped between the blade and the fence

without anything pushing it clear. A piece trapped like this is very likely to kick back at you.

Instead, use a stop-block alongside the fence to allow enough space for the cutoff piece so it cannot become trapped. For years I would grab a piece from the scrap bin to serve in this manner. Recently, however, I made the stop-block shown above. It didn't take long to make and is always ready when I need it.

This adjustable stop-block makes cutting short pieces safely a breeze. It clamps onto the rip fence to stay in place. The rip fence then provides coarse adjustment, while the $\frac{3}{8}$-16 carriage bolt handles fine adjustments. Each full turn moves the stop in or out $\frac{1}{16}$" (I filed a notch in the bolt head as a reference). The wing nut locks the adjustment in place.

■ JIG TIME

A Crosscut Sled

Crosscut sleds can be as elaborate or as simple as you like. I tend to lean toward the simple kind for two reasons. First, I'd rather spend my time in the shop building furniture rather than jigs. And second, with a simple jig, I don't mind modifying it if I must in order to accomplish some other task. A sled lends itself particularly well to modification, as you can screw any number of different fences or stop-blocks right to the base to help locate various workpieces. When the base has too many holes in it, simply build a new sled.

As for materials, I usually use whatever scrap I have on hand. I generally make the base from 1/2" or 3/4" plywood or MDF and the fences from straight 2×4s or other cheap wood. The sled in the drawing is just a suggestion; make yours to suit the pieces you are cutting and the materials you have to work with.

MATERIALS LIST inches							HARDWARE
REFERENCE	QUANTITY	PART	STOCK	THICKNESS	WIDTH	LENGTH	Assorted screws
A	1	base	plywood	3/4	28	32	
B	2	runners	hardwood	3/8	3/4	28	
C	1	front fence	pine 2×4	1 1/2	3 1/2	32	
D	1	rear fence	pine 2×4	1 1/2	3 1/2	32	
E	1	mounting cleats	hardwood	3/4	1 1/4	14	

MATERIALS LIST millimeters							HARDWARE
REFERENCE	QUANTITY	PART	STOCK	THICKNESS	WIDTH	LENGTH	Assorted screws
A	1	base	plywood	19	711	813	
B	2	runners	hardwood	10	19	711	
C	1	front fence	pine 2×4	38	89	813	
D	1	rear fence	pine 2×4	38	89	813	
E	1	mounting cleats	hardwood	19	32	356	

1 Cut the runners to fit snugly in the miter gauge slots. Drill and countersink screws about every 2" along each runner. Set the runners in the slots and place the base on top of them. Slide everything so the runners protrude over the front of the saw table. Screw the runners to the base through the first holes. Repeat at the rear of the table. Turn the assembly over and drive in the rest of the screws.

2 Screw the front fence to the leading edge of the sled to hold the two sides together after they are cut apart. Set the sled in place on the saw and make a cut through the base. Screw one end of the rear fence to the base. Adjust the fence so it is square to the saw kerf. Screw the other end in place through the oversize hole. Make a cut to check to make sure the fence is adjusted correctly, then add more screws to reinforce the connection.

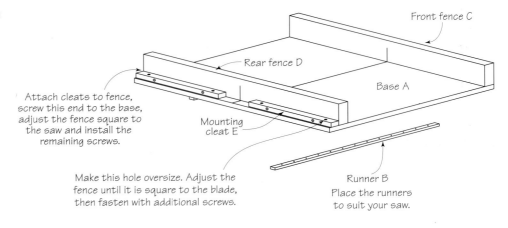

Front fence C

Rear fence D

Base A

Attach cleats to fence, screw this end to the base, adjust the fence square to the saw and install the remaining screws.

Mounting cleat E

Make this hole oversize. Adjust the fence until it is square to the blade, then fasten with additional screws.

Runner B
Place the runners to suit your saw.

joinery

IT PROBABLY COMES AS NO SURPRISE that you can use the table saw to cut an amazing variety of joinery. This includes some fairly simple joints, such as dadoes, as well as more involved joints, such as dovetails, box joints and mortise and tenons. The trick with most of these joints is to take advantage of the saw's ability to cut a straight line. With some of the joints, you'll need to build a jig to hold your stock in the right orientation to the blade. With others, careful attention to the setup is in order. As with all operations, you'll get the best results if your saw is well tuned and your blades are sharp.

■ *cutting dadoes and grooves*

Dadoes and grooves are square-bottomed cuts that do not go all the way through a board. The difference between a dado and a groove comes down to the way the cut is oriented in the wood. If the cut is made across the grain, it's a dado; if it is parallel to the grain, it's a groove. Other than that, there is no real difference in the way the cuts are made. To simplify this discussion, I'll refer to both cuts as grooves.

If you have a single groove to cut, the quickest method may be to simply set your regular saw blade for the proper depth and make multiple passes, shifting the workpiece slightly with each pass until the groove is the proper width. If you are using a rip or a combination blade with raker teeth, the bottom of your cut should be reasonably flat. However, if you are using a crosscut blade with an ATB (alternate tooth bevel) grind, the bottom of the groove is likely to be somewhat rough. If you have more than one groove to cut, this technique will quickly lose its charm. Then it's time to break out the dado head.

A dado head is pretty much just a fat saw blade. Two styles are available: the stack dado and the wobble dado. These can be adjusted to cut grooves from 1/4" to somewhat over 3/4" wide. The wobble dado is the less expensive but doesn't produce quite as nice a cut. Stack dadoes vary quite a bit in price from merely expensive to astronomical. How much to spend depends on what you intend to cut. Probably the most difficult material to cut a

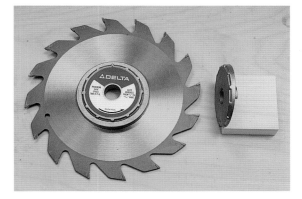

Wobble dadoes are adjusted by means of a pair of tapered plates that sandwich a single blade between them. By adjusting how much the blade is tilted on its axis, you can vary the width of the groove produced. Because of this "wobble," the bottom of the groove (especially on a wide cut) will be slightly deeper in the middle than it is at the edges.

A stack dado consists of two outer blades and a series of chippers that fit between them. Add or subtract chippers to make coarse adjustments. Most sets come with four or five 1/8"-thick chippers and a single 1/16"-thick chipper. You can make fine adjustments by adding shims in between the individual pieces.

groove in is hardwood-veneered plywood. If you routinely cut grooves in this material, spending more money on a dado head will save you some headaches.

Avoiding Expensive Dental Work

TOOL TALK

Be careful when changing your dado head (or any blade for that matter) not to set the blades down directly on the cast iron saw table. It is far too easy to damage the carbide teeth on the hard metal surface. Instead, keep a scrap of wood handy to serve as a work surface as you swap blades on and off the saw.

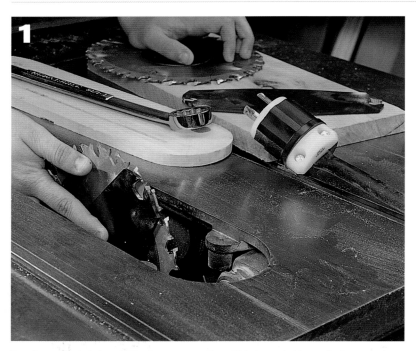

To set up a stack dado, add the necessary number of blades and chippers to the saw arbor. The two outer blades should always be on the outsides of the stack. Arrange the teeth on the chippers so they fall within the gullets on the outer blades and don't contact the teeth on adjacent chippers.

■ SAFETY FIRST

Dadoes and Guards

Because dado heads are rarely used to cut all the way through a board, you cannot use a splitter with one. In addition, because many blade covers are part of the splitter assembly, the cover cannot be used with the dado head either. This situation is not necessarily unsafe, because most of the time the board itself covers the dado head. However, you do want to be aware that the dado head will be exposed at the beginning and end of a cut. You should also be aware that a dado head (especially a stack dado setup for a wide cut) exerts a lot of force on the board. Make sure you have a secure grip on the workpiece as you push it past the blade.

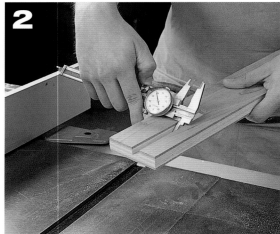

After tightening the nut to lock the dado head on the saw, cut a test piece. The piece can be guided with either the miter gauge or the rip fence, depending on the groove's orientation. Measure the width of the groove with a dial caliper. Add or subtract shims as required to achieve the desired result.

Precision Measurements

When I finally broke down and purchased a dial caliper, I was amazed at how useful it was. I had originally thought that measuring wood to the thousandth of an inch was ridiculous, but it is remarkable how much guesswork such precise measurements can save you. When shimming a dado set, for example, you can easily measure the original setting and add the exact thickness of shims required.

Shims

Several companies sell shim sets for stack dadoes. These consist of a series of plastic or metal discs of various thicknesses. These work quite well, but you can also make your own shims that do an admirable job. Plastic-coated playing cards are durable and are consistently 0.010" thick. Index cards (0.008") and Post-it notes (0.005") also have useful thicknesses. Even if you have a manufactured shim set, it is worth stocking a deck of cards and other types of paper to use as needed.

hot tip

cutting stopped grooves

At times you'll want to start (or stop) a groove in the middle of a board. If your workpiece is longer than 18" and you use the rip fence to guide your stock, this is a straightforward operation. You'll need to know where the front and the rear of the dado head are, and where on your workpiece you want the cut to start or stop. With this information in hand, you can set up some stop-blocks to help make the cut safe, accurate and repeatable.

Fasten a straight length of ¾" plywood to your rip fence. Ideally, the fence should be long enough so you can attach a stop at either end of the cut. Set the dado to the appropriate height.

Use a drafting triangle to help determine where the dado head meets the plane of the saw table at the front and back of the blade. Transfer these points to the face of the auxiliary fence. Lower the dado head below the surface of the saw table.

Mark where the cut should start and stop on the edge of the workpiece that will ride along the fence. Position the piece so the start mark aligns with the mark on the fence that indicates the rear of the blade. Clamp a stop-block to the fence at the trailing end of the board. Move the piece so the stop mark aligns with the other mark on the fence. Clamp a second stop-block at the leading edge of the board.

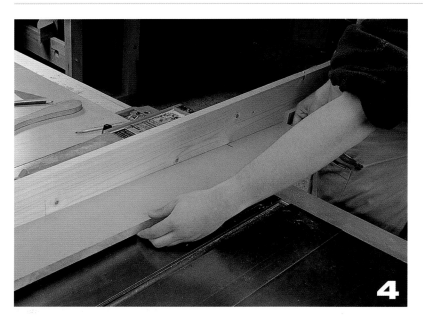

Reset the dado to its proper height. Hold the workpiece against the fence with its trailing edge against the stop-block. Start the saw and carefully lower the piece onto the blade. Once the piece is flat on the table, push it through the cut.

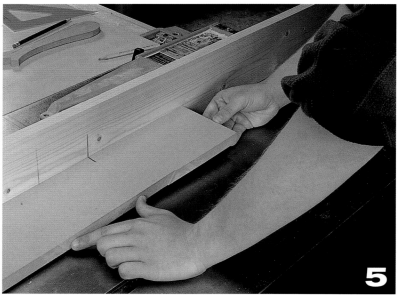

When the workpiece hits the second stop-block, carefully pivot it up and off the blade. Be sure to keep the piece pressed against the fence as you lift it.

cutting rabbets

A rabbet is a step cut in the edge of a board. Like a groove, a rabbet can be cut with or across the grain. You can cut a rabbet on the table saw in three ways. By setting the blade height to match the rabbet depth and shifting the fence slightly after each pass, you can create a rabbet with a regular saw blade. This grows tedious, however, if you have more than one piece to rabbet.

Another way to make a rabbet with a regular saw blade is to make the cut in two passes, first with the piece flat on the table, and then with the piece held on edge against the fence. If you have just a few pieces to rabbet, this saves you the trouble of setting up a dado.

The final way to rabbet is with a dado head. Rather than try to set up the dado to a specific width, it is far easier to make a rabbeting fence that covers part of the blade. With this setup you can expose only as much of the blade as you need. While rabbeting with a dado head involves more setup time, once the saw is set up, you can rabbet pieces as fast as you can push them past the blade.

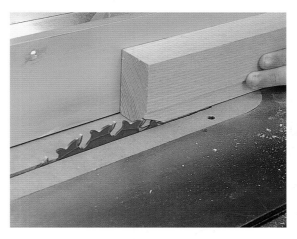

For a quick rabbet, set your regular saw blade to the appropriate depth and use the rip fence to guide the piece through the cut. Reposition the fence and make repeated passes until the rabbet is wide enough. The same technique works with a miter gauge equipped with an auxiliary fence and stop-block.

Rabbets can also be made with two saw cuts. As you complete the second cut, a small sliver of wood is likely to be cut free. Make sure this scrap is to the outside of the blade. If you trap it between the fence and the blade, it can come shooting back at you like a miniature spear.

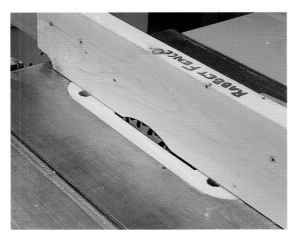

The fastest method of rabbeting (not counting the setup time) is to use a dado head and rabbeting fence. To make the fence, attach a piece of straight 2×6 to the rip fence. Set up the dado blade for its widest cut. Lower the dado and position the fence on top of it. Raise the dado into the fence to create a pocket.

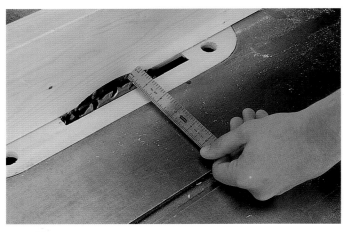

To set up the fence for rabbeting, set the dado head to the right height, then move the fence over until the necessary amount of the blade is exposed. This way you don't have to try to adjust the dado head to a specific width.

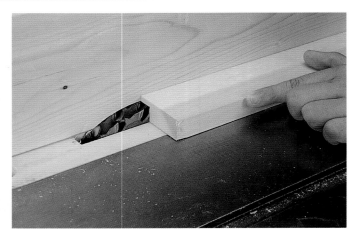

To cut rabbets with the grain, simply run the pieces along the fence.

To cut rabbets across the grain, guide the pieces with a miter gauge, using the fence as a stop. This is one of the few times it is safe to use the miter gauge and rip fence together. It works because there is no piece of scrap left over to kick back.

cutting tongue-and-groove joints

The tongue-and-groove joint is a connection where a thin tongue on one piece fits into a groove cut into another. There are a number of variations, including joints used to join pieces edge to edge, end to edge, and end to face. I use this last option a lot in building cabinets, both in plywood and solid stock. It's fast and easy to set up.

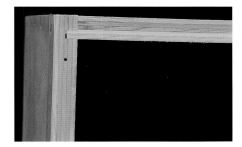

The tongue-and-groove joint is an excellent way to join the corners of plywood cabinet cases. It provides good alignment for the pieces and plenty of glue surface for a strong connection. Best of all, it is easy to set up and quick to cut. Using this joint, I can easily cut and assemble the cases for an entire kitchen in one day.

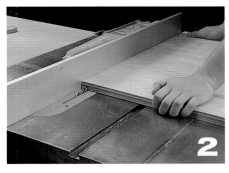

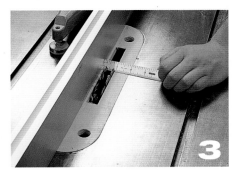

Start by cutting the 1/4"-wide grooves in the case sides. Set the height of the dado to approximately one-half the stock thickness. Set the rip fence by using a piece of the plywood as a gauge. You should just barely feel the teeth of the dado past the edge of the plywood.

Cut grooves in both the top and bottom edges of all the case sides. If you stack the pieces with the grooved side up, you'll be able to tell at a glance whether you've missed any of the cuts.

Reset the width of the dado head to approximately 5/8". Lower its height a little (1/32" +/-). This will leave a little space in the joint for trapped sawdust or other debris. Set the rip fence a little more than 1/4" from the blade.

Cut the tongues by running the pieces on edge past the blade. The initial cut should yield a tongue that is too big. Bump the fence over a tad and try again. Repeat until the tongue fits snugly in the groove. Sneaking up on the proper setting is easier than trying to set the fence using measurements.

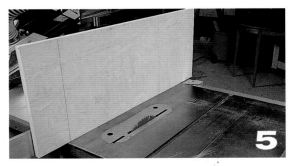

If cutting the pieces on edge makes you nervous, screw a piece of plywood to the fence to make the fence taller. Note: Cutting the pieces on edge makes for consistent tongues. Plywood varies enough in thickness that if you tried to cut the tongues with the pieces held flat, the fit would vary from too loose to too tight over a run of cabinets.

■ *cutting other tongue-and-groove joints*

As I mentioned earlier, the tongue-and-groove joint can also be used to join pieces end to edge and edge to edge. Edge-to-edge tongue-and-groove joinery is often used in flooring. End-to-edge tongue-and-groove joinery is used when making the frame for a frame and panel assembly. While a frame assembled with tongue-and-groove joints isn't as strong as one assembled with mortise-and-tenon joinery, it is certainly strong enough for most applications. I wouldn't assemble kitchen cabinet doors with tongue-and-groove joints (kitchen doors have to be as strong as possible to withstand constant use and abuse), but I've made plenty of small wall cabinets with tongue-and-groove door frames without any problem.

Whether you are going edge to edge, or end to edge, cut the groove first, then cut the tongue to match. In general, the width of the groove (and the thickness of the matching tongue) should be about one-third the thickness of the stock. The depth of the groove should be about twice its width. So, in 3/4" stock, the groove should be 1/4"-wide by 1/2"-deep.

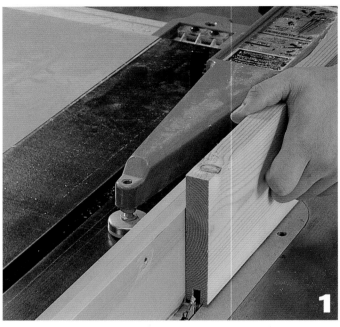

Set up a dado head to the proper depth and width. Set the rip fence so it is one-third the stock thickness away from the blade. Run all the pieces past the blade once. Then turn them around and run them again with the opposite face against the fence. This guarantees the grooves will be centered.

Leave the dado head set at the same height, but increase its width by 1/8". Attach the rabbeting fence to the rip fence. Rabbet both sides of a test piece. Start with most of the blade covered by the fence and gradually expose more until the tongue is a snug fit in the groove.

To cut a tongue on the end of a piece, use a tenoning jig like the one shown to help carry the piece past the blade. As discussed with the previous photo, start by making the tongue too big, then bump the fence over to adjust its size.

Reference Surfaces

Working from both faces of a board has both advantages and disadvantages. On the plus side, if you make a cut, then flip the board over and make a second cut, the tongue or groove you have just created will automatically be centered. However, if your material varies in thickness from piece to piece, referencing cuts from both faces of each piece will result in some of the tongues and grooves being either too big or too small. If you are not getting consistent results from the techniques described, try using a single surface as a reference. This concept is discussed in more depth in "Cutting Tenons" later in this chapter.

hot tip

■ JIG TIME

A Quick Tenoning Jig

While you can run a piece of stock on end past the blade with nothing more than a backer board to help push it, building this simple tenoning jig won't take much time and takes almost all of the risk out of the operation. The jig itself is made from two pieces of plywood or other sheet stock. The toggle clamp shown in photo three is optional. It takes away all the worry about securing the pieces, but it also slows down the operation. Use the rip fence on your saw to position and guide the jig.

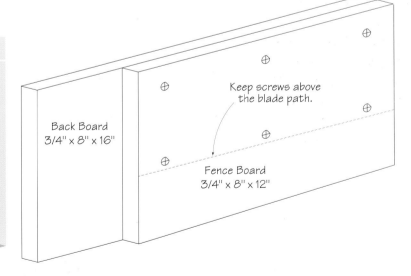

Back Board
3/4" x 8" x 16"

Keep screws above the blade path.

Fence Board
3/4" x 8" x 12"

■ *making a lock joint*

The lock joint is a variation of a tongue-and-groove joint that can be used to join the corners of drawers and other boxes. While it lacks the strength and panache of dovetails or box joints, it is still quite serviceable and relatively easy to cut. The photos show the joint being cut for a drawer with a $3/4$"-thick front and $1/2$"-thick sides. With a little thought, you can easily adapt the techniques shown to other thicknesses of material.

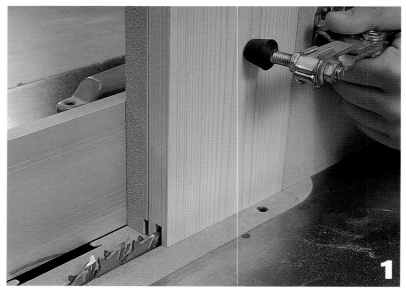

Set up your dado head to make a $1/4$"-wide cut. Position the rip fence so the face of the quick tenoning jig is $1/4$" away from the blade. Set the blade height to match the thickness of the drawer sides ($1/2$"). Cut the end of a test piece, using the jig to guide the piece through the cut.

Measure to make sure the thickness of the resulting tongue (the one on the side of the piece that was against the fence) matches the width of the groove. Adjust the fence and make additional test cuts as needed. When the setup is correct, cut the drawer fronts.

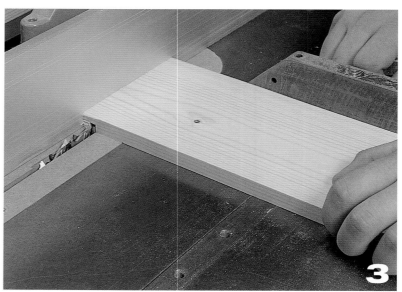

Reset the height of the dado head to one-half the thickness of the drawer sides. Position the rip fence as a stop and cut a groove across a test piece. The distance between the blade and the fence should match the width of the groove. Reset the fence as needed, then cut the grooves in the drawer sides.

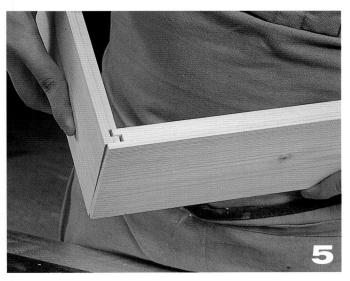

The final step is to cut one of the tongues on each end of the drawer fronts short. Set a stop along a miter gauge extension fence to govern the length of the tongue. Start by cutting the tongue too long, then adjust until it is a perfect fit in the drawer side. Cut all the drawer fronts.

The joint should fit together with a minimum of fuss. Add glue and a few reinforcing nails when you are ready for the final assembly.

Drawer Joinery

The lock joint is an excellent joint for joining a drawer front to the sides. It hides the end grain on the sides, and the overlap adds strength to the assembly. To join the drawer back to the drawer sides, the lock joint is not necessary. As shown in the photo, a simple groove cut in each side will house the drawer back just fine. With the addition of glue and two or three reinforcing nails, you will quickly be able to assemble many drawers.

■ *cutting box joints*

The box joint, also known as the finger or comb joint, is an incredibly strong corner joint that is perfectly suited to the table saw. The joint consists of a series of inter-locking pins. It is cut with a dado head in conjunction with a shop-made jig. Once you have made and adjusted the jig, the joint requires only a quick setup. I am amazed every time I pull my jig off the shelf and put it on the saw: The joints it makes fit just right without my having to fuss with the adjustments at all.

When you set up to cut box joints, the first decision to make is how wide to make the pins. There are two factors to consider here: appearance and strength. The thinner the pins, the more of them there will be. More pins equals more glue surface equals more strength. However, thin pins may look a little goofy if you are working with particularly large stock — the sides of a blanket chest, for example. So, a little compromise is involved. Here's what I do: For drawers and boxes (which I almost always make from stock that is $1/2$" or less thick), I use $1/4$"-wide pins; this is what my box joint jig is set up for. On the rare occasions that I cut box joints in thicker (or wider) stock, I move up to $1/2$"- or even $3/4$"-wide pins and I build a jig specifically for the job.

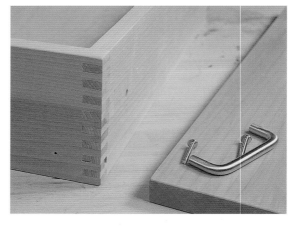

While the box joint lacks the sophisti-cated look of the dovetail, it is every bit as strong, and suitable in the same applications. I often use box joints to assemble the drawers for kitchen cabinets as well as the occa-sional jewelry box.

Set up a dado head to match the width of the pins you desire. The height of the dado should be slightly less than the stock thickness. Mark the top edge of all the pieces. As you cut, the marked edges should always point to the right. Hold the first piece tight against the jig's key and push the jig past the blade to cut the slot.

Move the piece over, so the slot you just cut is now over the pin. Cut the next slot. Keep going like this until you have cut slots across the width of the piece.

3

The mating piece starts with a slot. To position it, slip the first piece over the key with the marked edge facing to the left. Butt the marked edge of the mating piece up to the first piece. Make the cut. Remove the first piece and slide the second piece over against the key to position it for the next cut. Continue making slots across the width of the board.

4

Cutting box joints goes pretty quickly. Once you are confident in your jig and your technique, you can make the process even more efficient by ganging the pieces as you cut them.

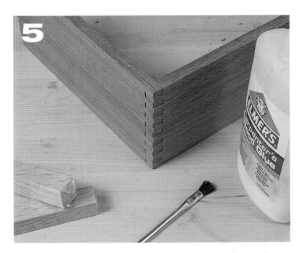

5

By keeping the dado height less than the stock thickness, the pins will be slightly recessed from the faces of the pieces when assembled. This means you can get direct clamp pressure on the joints when gluing up. Wrap your clamp blocks with plastic packing tape to prevent them from being glued in place.

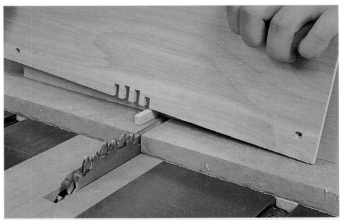

Calling for Back Up

hot tip

If you find your workpieces are splintering badly on the back side of the cut, it may be because the slot in the jig is too tall and the wood fibers don't have adequate support. You can fix this easily by using a sacrificial piece of $1/4$" plywood behind your workpieces. To cut the initial slot in the sacrificial piece, remove the key from the jig.

■ JIG TIME

Box Joint Jig

To cut box joints, you need to make a box joint jig. The jig shown here is a design I've been refining for the past twenty years. It works well, yielding consistent results even after sitting on a shelf for months at a time. If you are pressed for space, you could just make the two-part, adjustable fence system and simply screw it to your miter gauge when you need it. However, I think the jig will hold its adjustment better if you build the sled, too.

The key to this jig's success is literally a key — the small piece of wood projecting from the front fence — and its position relative to the blade. Make the key from a durable hardwood such as maple or cherry. Start with a piece that is slightly too big and scrape or sand it until it is a snug fit in its slot. I never glue the key in my jig as I want to be able to replace it easily should it wear. Note: The back fence is the one with the slotted hole. The front fence just has a counterbored hole. This makes it easier to replace the front fence when necessary. As you build the jig, be sure to keep the fences square to the blade. This can be accomplished by attaching the fence with one screw at first, then adjusting it as necessary before driving in the rest of the screws. The fences should also be perpendicular to the base. Make adjustments by adding shims between the fence and the blade guard.

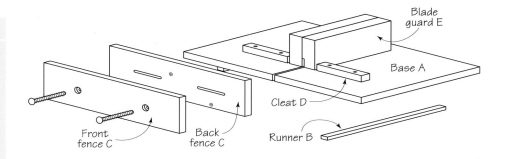

Blade guard E

Base A

Cleat D

Front fence C

Back fence C

Runner B

Fence Detail

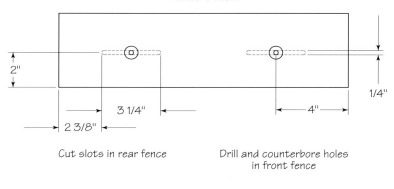

2"

1/4"

2 3/8"

3 1/4"

4"

Cut slots in rear fence

Drill and counterbore holes in front fence

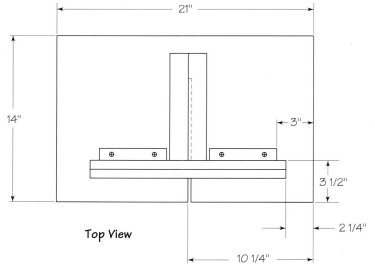

21"

14"

3"

3 1/2"

2 1/4"

10 1/4"

Top View

MATERIALS LIST inches

REFERENCE	QUANTITY	PART	STOCK	THICKNESS	WIDTH	LENGTH
A	1	base	plywood	3/4	14	21
B	2	runners	hardwood	3/8	3/4	14
C	2	fences	hardwood	3/4	4 1/4	16
D	2	cleats	hardwood	3/4	1	5 1/2
E	2	blade guards	pine 2×4	1 1/2	3 1/2	9

MATERIALS LIST millimeters

REFERENCE	QUANTITY	PART	STOCK	THICKNESS	WIDTH	LENGTH
A	1	base	plywood	19	356	533
B	2	runners	hardwood	10	19	356
C	2	fences	hardwood	19	108	406
D	2	cleats	hardwood	19	25	140
E	2	blade guards	pine 2×4	38	89	229

HARDWARE

2 Carriage bolts with washers and wing nuts
$1/4 - 20 \times 2$"

Assorted screws

HARDWARE

2 Carriage bolts with washers and wing nuts
$6 - 508 \times 51$mm

Assorted screws

How Tight?

As you adjust your box joint jig, you may discover that what seems like the proper adjustment for a 2"- or 3"-wide board doesn't work for an 8"- or 9"-wide board. This is because any errors in the setup is compounded as you progress across a board. For example, if the jig is misaligned by $1/16$", the first cut will be off by $1/16$", the second will be off by $1/8$" ($1/16$" + $1/16$") and so on. In theory, there is one right setting. In practice, the right setting depends on the width of the pieces you are joining. The wider the pieces, the closer you have to be to that one "perfect" setting.

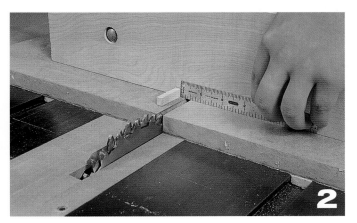

To cut the slot for the key, set up dado to match the width of the pins you intend to cut. Set the height to 3/8". Shift the adjustable fence over almost all the way to the left. Cut the slot.

Cut a key that is a snug fit in the slot, then chamfer its top edges. Shift the fence to the right so the distance between the key and the blade equals the width of the dado blade. Make a test joint. If the joint is too tight, move the key closer to the blade. If it is too loose, move the key away from the blade.

cutting dovetails

The dovetail is perhaps the classic wood-working corner joint. It consists of pins cut in one board, that mate with tails cut in another. On the pin board, the angles are visible from the end, while on the tail board, the angles are visible from the face. Traditionally, the pins are fairly narrow and the tails somewhat wider. These days, many woodworkers turn to the router along with any of a number of different jigs to handle their dovetailing needs. Before you invest in such tooling, consider that the table saw does a surprisingly good job of cutting through-dovetails. Actually, it isn't that surprising when you consider that the secret to cutting dovetails is being able to saw straight. If there is one thing a table saw does well, it is to saw a straight line.

Table-sawn dovetails look very much like those that were cut by hand. You can vary the spacing to accommodate different width boards, although the joints are easiest to make if you make the pins and the tails uniform sizes. Once you make the setup, all the pieces you cut using it should be interchangeable, making a production run quite easy to accomplish.

Dovetailing on the table saw is both easier and more complicated than cutting box joints. It is easier because there is no jig involved. You just need an auxiliary fence for your miter gauge, a stop-block and a series of spacers. However, dovetailing involves at least three separate setups as opposed to the box joint's one.

The through-dovetail, where the end grain of each board is visible, is a strong way to join pieces together. The table saw method shown here gives you a lot of freedom in the size and layout of the pins and tails.

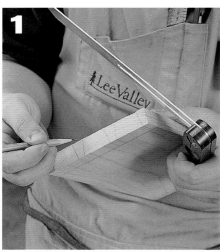

Cut your pieces to width and square their ends. Lay out the pins on the end of one piece. Start with a half pin on either side, then fill in with as many pins as you want in between. The distance from pin center to pin center should be equal, as should the width of the narrow side of each pin.

Note: This technique is a slick one. While the process may seem confusing at first, once you actually start cutting, it will become clear.

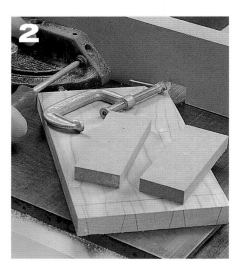

Cut one spacer for each full pin. The width of the spacers should equal the distance from pin center to pin center. (I use $1/2$" MDF for spacer material.) Sand the corners lightly to remove any fuzz so the spacers fit closely together. Attach an auxiliary fence to your miter gauge. For most work, a fence 3" wide and 24" long will be fine. Center the fence on the blade.

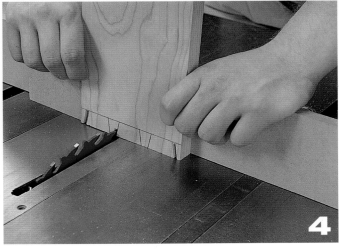

Lay out the cut line for the first half pin on the tail board. Tilt your saw blade to 10°. Hold the tail board against the fence and align the cut line with the blade. Position the spacers next to the tail board. Clamp a stop-block to the fence at the far end of the spacers. The spacers and stop-block should be away from the direction the blade tilts.

Scribe a line across the tail board to indicate the shoulder line for the joint. Set the blade height so the cut stops just below this line. With all the spacers in place, make the first cut, then pivot the board side to side and make the second cut. Remove the first spacer and repeat, then remove the second spacer, and so on. Once all the cuts are made, carefully cut away the remaining waste, positioning the board by eye.

Why 10°

hot tip

Oftentimes, the dovetail angle is expressed as a ratio (usually somewhere between 5:1 and 8:1). If you draw these ratios out (moving over 1" and up both 5" and 8", then connecting the dots) you'll discover 10° falls somewhere in between. I like the way it looks, but feel free to vary it if you so desire.

The one bit of handwork you'll have to do is to trim the shoulder line of the tail board. (To avoid this, see "A Dovetail Blade," above.) Use a sharp chisel to trim away the steps left by the saw blade. Be particularly careful when trimming the shoulders for the half pins, as these are especially visible in the finished joint.

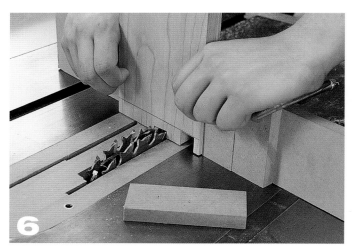

Reset the saw blade to 0° and exchange the blade for a ¾" dado head (or a dado that is a little narrower than the small dimension of the tails). Set the blade height to match the shoulder line of the joint. Set the miter gauge so it is at an angle of 80° when measured to the right side of the blade. Clamp a stop-block to the fence to position the pin board for the first cut. Make the cut then add the spacers in turn for the next cuts.

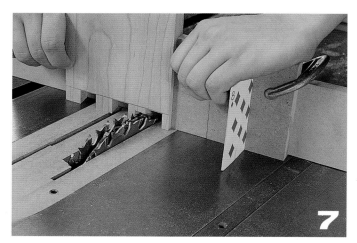

Reset the miter gauge so it is at 80° to the blade when measured to the left. Position the pin board to cut the second half pin. Err to the side of making the pin too wide. Butt the spacers against the pin board and clamp a stop-block beside the spacers as a reference point. Make the cuts and check the pins' fit in the tail board. Add paper shims (see "Shims" earlier in this chapter) beside the stop-block to make the pins smaller.

Allowing for Glue-Up

When I cut my dovetails, I set the depth of cut slightly less than the thickness of the stock. This means when the pieces go together, the end grain will be slightly recessed. This allows me to squeeze the joint together with a clamp and a clamping block without having to worry about the overlapping pieces holding the joint apart. I wrap my clamping blocks with plastic tape to keep them from sticking to the glue.

hot tip

■ *cutting tenons*

The table saw also plays an important role in cutting that other venerable joint, the mortise and tenon. In this joint, a long tongue (the tenon) cut on the end of one piece fits into a slot (the mortise) cut in the edge (or face) of another.

While mortising on the table saw is out of the question (except for the open mortise-and-tenon or slip joint, discussed later in this chapter), the table saw does an excellent job of cutting tenons. For the best results, hold the pieces on end as you cut them. To make these cuts, you'll need a tenoning jig. For the occasional run of tenons, the quick tenoning jig, shown earlier in this chapter, will be fine. However, if you do a lot of mortise-and-tenon work, the more elaborate model, as described later in this chapter, offers better adjustability and ease of use.

The tenoning jig I designed for this book is a refinement of a design I have used for the past few years. It can accommodate a wide variety of pieces (even curved ones, as shown on the cover). One of its key features is the adjustable reference plate. This allows you to set a reference point in relationship to the piece you are cutting, and then use a spacer to move the piece over a specific amount so as to cut the perfect thickness of tenon. Once you match the spacer to the width of the mortise you can count on the jig turning out snug-fitting tenons day after day.

As for the mortises, I think the easiest

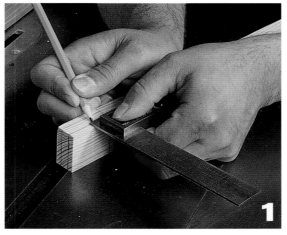

Start by laying out the tenon on the end of one of your workpieces. Extend the cut lines so you can see them on all four sides of the piece. Mark one face of each workpiece. Make sure when you load the pieces into the jig, the marked face is against the jig.

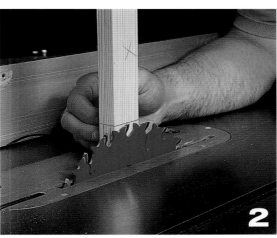

Set the blade height to match the length of the tenon. As these cuts are essentially rip cuts, use a rip blade to make them. This is particularly helpful if your saw is on the underpowered side and/or the tenons are especially long.

Clamp the workpiece in the jig. Slide the adjustable base over until the blade aligns with the cut line that is away from the jig. Lock the base in place, then slide the reference base against the adjustable base and lock it in place, too. Make the first cut.

way to cut them is with a plunge router, although a hollow chisel mortiser also does an admirable job. Whichever way you choose, you'll want to cut the mortises first, then match your tenons to them.

TOOL TALK

Dualing Blades

By inserting a spacer between a pair of matched rip blades, you can make both tenon cheek cuts at the same time. Delta makes a spacer kit (model #34-171) just for this purpose. Adjust the exact width of the spacer with shims to make the resulting tenon fit in your mortise.

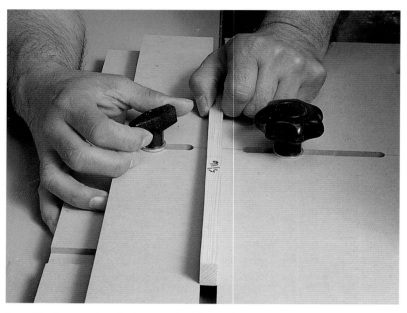

To position the workpiece for the second cut, loosen the adjustable base and sandwich a spacer between the adjustable base and the reference base. For details regarding the spacer see "Making the Tenoning Jig" later in this chapter. Make the second cut.

Reposition the adjustable base to make the edge cuts. The exact placement of these cuts isn't as critical as it is for the side cuts. Rather than messing with the clamp, hand-hold the pieces for this operation.

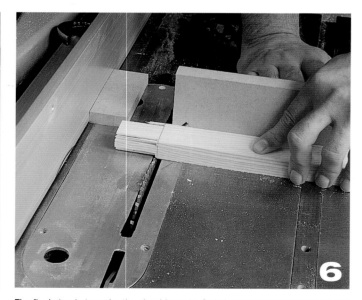

The final step is to make the shoulder cuts. Switch to a crosscut blade and set the blade height so it barely scores the tenon surface. Guide the piece past the blade with a miter gauge. Position the rip fence along with a stop-block to control the length of the tenon.

cutting tenons with a dado cutter

Using a tenoning jig to cut tenons works very well. The jig is, however, time-consuming to build and time-consuming to set up. If tenoning is a once-in-a-blue-moon operation for you, the hassle involved in the jig, and its subsequent storage, is probably not worth the bother. Instead, cut your tenons as though you were cutting extra wide rabbets. Set up a dado blade and guide the pieces past it with a miter gauge. Position the rip fence to control the tenon length; there is no appreciable kickback risk as there is no scrap piece to get caught.

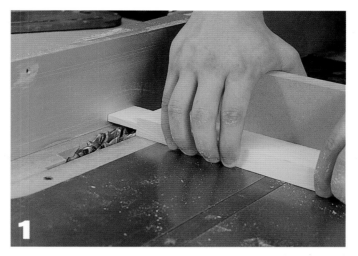

To cut a tenon with a dado blade, hold the workpiece flat on the table and push it past the blade with the miter gauge. Flip the piece over to cut the other side. The tenon thickness is controlled by the height of the blade. Because you are cutting from both sides of your workpiece, keep in mind that any adjustment to the blade height will be doubled on the workpiece.

Because cutting tenons with a dado blade doesn't yield especially precise results, leave the tenons a little thick. Pare them to a precise fit with either a rabbet plane or a sharp chisel. This gives you a chance to even out any irregularities left by the dado, and to compensate for any trouble caused by variations in the thickness of the stock. Note: The holding device is a handy little thing called a bench hook.

■ *cutting slip joints*

The slip joint is a variation of the mortise-and-tenon joint that can be cut entirely on the table saw. While the exposed areas of end grain make it less visually appealing than a true mortise and tenon, it is one of the strongest methods of joining the corners of a frame together. It is also relatively fast to cut as it involves fewer setups. As with most mortise-and-tenon joinery, you should start by cutting the center slot (or open mortise). Then you can cut the tenon to match.

The checkerboard pattern on this frame and panel door is a hallmark of the slip joint used to join the corners. While the traditional mortise and tenon has a cleaner look, the slip joint has a lot more glue surface, which makes it quite strong.

The width of the mortise should be about one-third the thickness of the stock. For example, in 3/4" material, make the mortise 1/4" to 5/16" wide. Adjust the blade height to match the width of the adjoining piece. Set the adjustable base to center the mortise in the workpiece.

The tenon is cut in two passes. You can clamp the mortised piece in the jig to help position the adjustable base for these cheek cuts. If your dado leaves a nice crisp shoulder, you can assemble the joint right from here. Otherwise you'll need to make separate shoulder cuts so the joint goes together cleanly.

If you need to clean up the shoulders, switch to a crosscut blade. Set the depth of cut so the blade barely scores the tenon cheeks. Guide the pieces through the cut with the miter gauge, using the rip fence to control the tenon length.

When gluing up a slip joint, applying pressure perpendicular to the glue surfaces makes for the best glue bond. If necessary, you can also use clamps to seat the pieces against their respective shoulders.

Making the Tenoning Jig

This is the most complicated jig I've ever devised. It came about for a couple of reasons. One, I needed something really slick for the cover of the book, and two, I wanted to present a truly reliable device for tenoning on the table saw. I built this jig and shipped it out to the folks at Popular Woodworking Books so they could photograph it for the cover. Then they sent it back and I started using it. After a couple of tenons, I realized the jig needed some changes, so what you see here is the revised version. It works quite well.

The main change I made to the jig was to cut the adjustable base into two pieces. This created a piece I call the reference base. You can move it to provide a reference point from which to make adjustments. You can also make spacers that fit between the reference base and the adjustable base to cut specific-size tenons. These spacers are simply strips of wood that are cut to a precise thickness.

Construction is pretty straightforward, with all the pieces screwed together. Start by making the two bases and the tracks in between. Take your time when adding the braces to make sure that the vertical table ends up truly square to the saw table. Where bolts are involved, I mortised the heads into the surfaces to keep them from turning. You could just as easily use carriage bolts. The slots were cut with a table-mounted router. The dimensions are not especially critical. As I was designing this jig, I tried to think of every situation where I might want to use it, and then built it with that in mind. Use the materials you have on hand and your jig will work just fine. Just be sure to keep the screws away from the blade's path.

I used a commercial runner to fit in the miter gauge slot. I saw it in the Woodcraft catalog and decided to give it a try. It works very well. I am tempted to order some more to replace the runners on my other sleds.

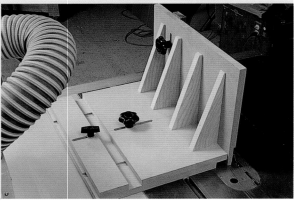

REFERENCE	QUANTITY	PART	STOCK	THICKNESS	WIDTH	LENGTH	COMMENTS
A	2	bases	plywood	3/4	13	18	one of these is cut later into the adjustable base and the reference base after the runners are attached
B	2	runners	hardwood	3/16	3/4	13	
C	1	vertical table	plywood	3/4	12	18 1/2	
D	4	braces	hardwood	3/4	3 1/4	9	
E	1	fence	hardwood	3/4	2	14	make several; they get cut up as you use the jig

MATERIALS LIST inches

HARDWARE

INCRA runner — Woodcraft #14V59

Assorted screws

Bolts — 3/8 – 16 × 2"

Knobs — Woodcraft #142225

MATERIALS LIST millimeters

REFERENCE	QUANTITY	PART	STOCK	THICKNESS	WIDTH	LENGTH	COMMENTS
A	2	bases	plywood	19	330	457	one of these is cut later into the adjustable base and the reference base after the runners are attached
B	2	runners	hardwood	5	19	330	
C	1	vertical table	plywood	19	305	470	
D	4	braces	hardwood	19	82	229	
E		fence	hardwood	19	51	356	make several; they get cut up as you use the jig

HARDWARE

INCRA runner — Woodcraft #14V59

Assorted screws

Bolts — 10 – 406 × 2"

Knobs — Woodcraft #142225

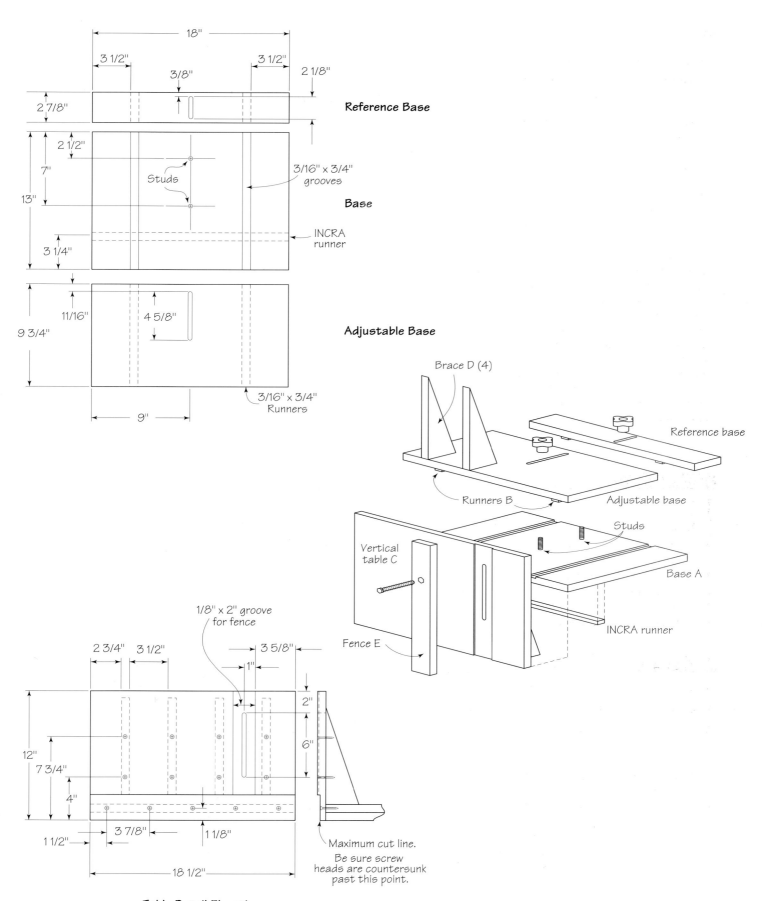

Reference Base

Base

18"

3 1/2"

3/8"

3 1/2"

2 1/8"

2 7/8"

2 1/2"

7"

13"

3 1/4"

Studs

3/16" x 3/4" grooves

INCRA runner

11/16"

9 3/4"

4 5/8"

9"

3/16" x 3/4" Runners

Adjustable Base

Brace D (4)

Reference base

Runners B

Adjustable base

Studs

Vertical table C

Base A

Fence E

INCRA runner

2 3/4" 3 1/2"

1/8" x 2" groove for fence

3 5/8"

1"

2"

12"

7 3/4"

6"

4"

1 1/2"

3 7/8"

1 1/8"

18 1/2"

Maximum cut line. Be sure screw heads are countersunk past this point.

Table Detail Elevation

cutting miter joints

At face value, the miter joint ought to be about as simple a joint to cut as can be. Simply saw the adjoining pieces at an angle (usually 45°) and you're done. But it rarely seems to work out that way. Either the pieces slip or the angle setting isn't quite right, and suddenly what should be simple has turned into a big mess.

Actually, to call the miter a joint at all is a little misleading. By itself, the miter is a lousy joint because there is no overlap, no places with good long-grain-to-long-grain glue surface, and thus no real strength. So, without some kind of reinforcement the miter is at best a fancy butt joint. Miters can also be tricky to glue up because they lack positive shoulders to keep the pieces in line, plus it can be difficult to get clamping pressure across the joint where you need it.

Now I am not saying the miter is not without its uses. From a designer's point of view, it is a marvelous thing because it allows the grain patterns or moulding profiles to wrap around a corner without interruption. This makes for a clean look. But to accomplish that clean look takes some effort.

There are a number of ways to cut miters, depending on the orientation of the cut in the workpiece. At the corners of simple frames, cut miters by pivoting the miter gauge to the appropriate angle. This method can be greatly improved by adding an auxiliary fence and a special stop-block to the miter gauge. For miters at the corners of boxes or cases, tilt the saw blade while leaving the miter gauge set square. For compound miters, tilt the blade and pivot the miter gauge. And for miters in crown moulding, tilt the moulding and pivot the miter gauge.

A Miter Stop Block

When mitering the second end of a frame member, it is nice to be able to butt the first end up against a stop-block. But when the first end of the piece is mitered, there isn't much surface there to have in contact with the block. Plus you run the risk of damaging the fragile point at the end of the miter. This stop-block remedies this by providing a metal point to contact the mitered surface. Grind the point on the end of a $\frac{1}{4}$" × 3" bolt. Insert a T-nut in the stop-block to provide the threads. A second nut serves to lock the bolt in position. Make adjustments by advancing or retracting the bolt.

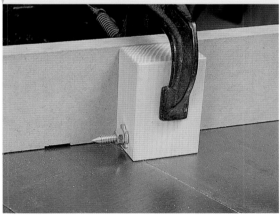

Attach an auxiliary fence to your miter gauge. Set the miter gauge to the appropriate angle in relation to the blade. I use a T-bevel in conjunction with a layout tool called an Angle Boss to get the angle right. Or, you could set the T-bevel against a combination square or a rule with a protractor head.

Hold the workpiece against the auxiliary fence. Clamp a stop-block at its end so you can hold the piece against the block to keep it from slipping as you cut.

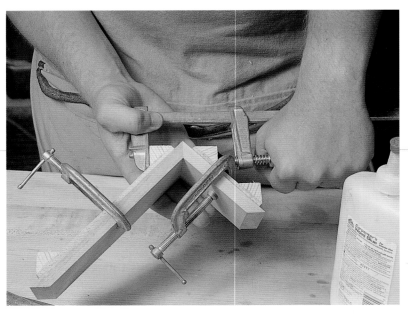

Cut miters across the width of a workpiece with the stock held flat on the table and the blade tilted to the appropriate angle. For small pieces, such as those for a box, use the miter gauge along with an auxiliary fence and a stop-block as a guide. For wider pieces, such as those for a cabinet side, guide the pieces along the rip fence.

Gluing up a mitered box or cabinet can be a tricky affair. I have the best luck when I have made angled glue blocks that match the angle of the miter. Mount these to a piece of $1/4''$ plywood that you can clamp to the workpiece. The angle allows you to apply pressure directly perpendicular to the joint.

If you want to build a box with sides that splay in or out, you'll need to cut compound miters at the corners. To cut a compound miter, tilt the blade and pivot the miter gauge. The compound miter settings chart on the next page shows the angles needed for varying degrees of splay for 4-, 6- and 8-sided constructions. Be sure to test your setup with scrap stock before committing good wood.

To complete the second miter cut, either reset the miter gauge to measure the same angle in the opposite direction, or place the workpiece on the opposite side of the blade, turning the workpiece over so the opposite face is down on the table and the opposite edge is against the gauge.

CHART compound miter settings

| Side Tilt | 4-SIDED CONSTRUCTION | | 6-SIDED CONSTRUCTION | | 8-SIDED CONSTRUCTION | |
	Blade Tilt	Miter Gauge	Blade Tilt	Miter Gauge	Blade Tilt	Miter Gauge
0 (VERTICAL)	45 (TO THE TABLE)	90 (TO THE BLADE)	60	90	67.5	90
5	45.25	85	60.25	87.5	67.75	88
10	45.75	80.25	60.5	84.5	68	86
15	46.75	75.5	61	81.75	68.5	84
20	48.25	71.25	61.75	79	69	82
25	50	67	62.75	76.5	69.75	80
30	52.25	63.5	64	74	70.5	78.25
35	54.75	60.25	65.5	71.75	71.75	76.75
40	57.5	57.25	67.25	69.75	73	75
45	60	54.75	69	67.75	74.25	73.75
50	63	52.5	71	66.25	75.75	72.5
55	66	50.75	73.25	64.75	77.5	71.25
60	69	49	75.5	63.5	79	70.25

To find the blade tilt setting for your table saw's blade angle gauge, subtract the blade tilt angle in the chart from 90°.

reinforcing miter joints

Once the miters are cut (and in some cases glued together first) they need to be reinforced or they will eventually fall apart. You can accomplish this in a number of ways. Two of the fastest are nails and biscuits, but because this is a table saw book, I won't go into the details about those methods. Two table saw techniques, however, will do the trick. The first involves running a spline the length of the miter. The spline will be almost invisible after the joint is assembled. With the second method, the groove for the spline is cut after the joint is glued together. These splines will be visible and can add a nice visual element to your work.

For a "hidden" spline, cut a groove in the pieces perpendicular to the miter's face. The closer you can keep the groove to the inside corner, the deeper the groove can be. For 3/4" material, a 1/8" groove (a regular saw kerf) will be fine. For thicker material, you may want to increase the width of the groove to 1/4" or more.

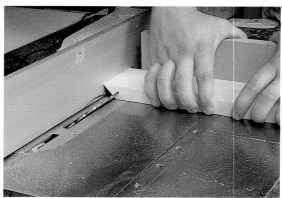

For a 45° miter you can run the pieces flat on the saw table, guided by the miter gauge. Use the rip fence to help keep the grooves placed consistently. For compound miter cuts, the only way to keep the groove perpendicular to the miter face is to run the pieces past the blade vertically. Attach the pieces to the tenoning jig to keep the groove placement consistent and to protect the fragile tip of the miter.

By cutting the spline grooves after assembly, you create an opportunity to add a decorative element to your project. Try adding splines made of contrasting wood to emphasize what is happening at the joint.

Make a quick carriage to help support the assembly as you move it past the blade. The blade height should be just shy of the joint's inside corner. For flat frames, you can saw right through the carriage's supporting pieces. Just be sure no screws are in the path of the blade.

Spline Grain Direction

The grain in the splines should run across the joint for maximum strength. For a hidden spline, this means the length of the piece will be only about 3/4", while the width will be considerably more. Rather than try to cut such a short, wide piece, I make the splines from fairly narrow pieces and use as many as necessary to fill the groove.

hot tip

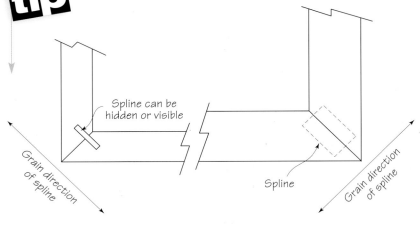

Spline can be hidden or visible

Grain direction of spline

Spline

Grain direction of spline

■ JIG TIME

The Spline Carriage

The spline carriage is another quick jig you can assemble in a matter of minutes. Cut the two angled fences so the included angle matches that of the pieces you will be cutting. For a square corner, the two fences are cut at 45°. Fasten the fences to the carrier board with screws. Be sure to keep the screws above the blade's path.

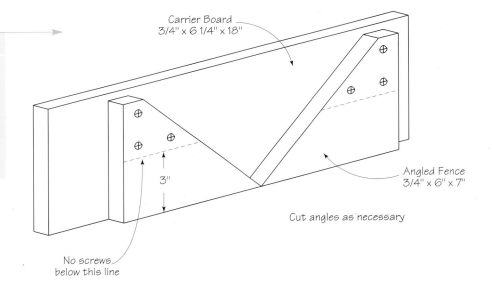

Carrier Board
3/4" x 6 1/4" x 18"

Angled Fence
3/4" x 6" x 7"

Cut angles as necessary

3"

No screws below this line

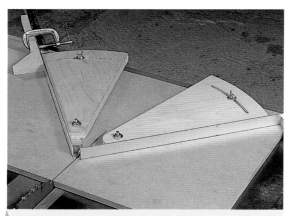

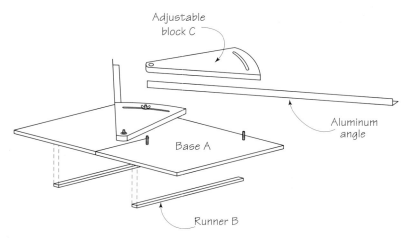

Adjustable block C

Aluminum angle

Base A

Runner B

The Miter Sled

This miter sled is worth the effort to make if you cut miters on a regular basis. One of the key features is how forgiving the jig is. As long as the two fences are square to one another, the resulting miter cuts will make a square corner, regardless of whether or not the fences are set at exactly 45° to the blade. The two sides can be adjusted independently, as well, which makes it possible to join mouldings of unequal width in a perfect miter. This is necessary sometimes, believe me!

Construction is similar to that for a crosscut sled. Start by attaching the runners to the base, then make the adjustable blocks and attach the aluminum angle. The curved slots are cut with a router: Fasten the router at one end of a 20" piece of $\frac{1}{4}$" plywood. Chuck a $\frac{1}{4}$" bit in the router and plunge it through the plywood. Drill a $\frac{1}{4}$" hole in the block at the pivot point, then drill a $\frac{1}{4}$" hole in the plywood $10\frac{1}{2}$" away from the bit. Use the router like a giant compass to cut the curved slots. Rabbet the undersides of the adjustable blocks to receive the aluminum angle.

hot tip

Sled Plan View

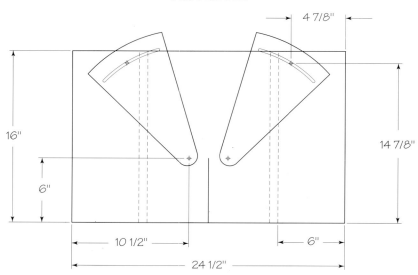

4 7/8"

16"

6"

14 7/8"

10 1/2"

6"

24 1/2"

Adjustable Block Detail

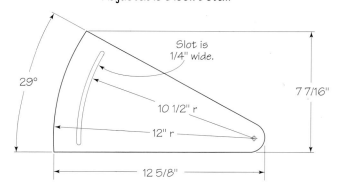

Slot is 1/4" wide.

29°

10 1/2" r

12" r

7 7/16"

12 5/8"

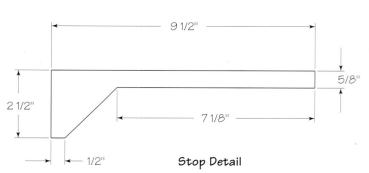

9 1/2"

2 1/2"

5/8"

7 1/8"

1/2"

Stop Detail

REFERENCE	QUANTITY	PART	STOCK	THICKNESS	WIDTH	LENGTH
A	1	base	plywood	$1/2$	16	$24^{1}/2$
B	2	runners	hardwood	$3/8$	$3/4$	16
C	2	adjustable blocks	hardwood	$3/4$	$7^{5}/8$	$13^{1}/2$
D	2	stops	hardwood	$3/4$	$2^{1}/2$	$9^{1}/2$

HARDWARE

4 — $1/4$ – 20 × $2^{1}/2$" carriage bolts with washers and wing nuts

2 — $3/4$" × $3/4$" × 24" aluminum angle

Assorted screws

REFERENCE	QUANTITY	PART	STOCK	THICKNESS	WIDTH	LENGTH
A	1	base	plywood	13	406	623
B	2	runners	hardwood	10	19	406
C	2	adjustable blocks	hardwood	19	194	343
D	2	stops	hardwood	19	64	242

HARDWARE

4 — 6 – 508 × 64mm carriage bolts with washers and wing nuts

2 — 19mm × 19mm × 610mm aluminum angle

Assorted screws

If you cut a lot of miters — for picture frames, for example — you may find it handy to build a miter sled. This model features two adjustable heads, one on either side of the blade. Adjust the heads so they are square to one another and you won't have to worry about the exact angle they make with the blade. Cut one end of each frame piece on the left side, then cut the other end to length and to the proper angle on the right. Set the adjustable stops for repeatability and to help keep the pieces from slipping.

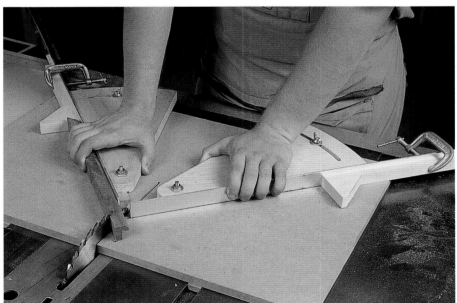

shaping

WITH ALL THE WORK YOU CAN accomplish on a table saw, simply cutting pieces to size and making joints, it is easy to overlook the saw's capabilities as a shaping machine. This would be a shame, because the table saw is an awesome performer when it comes to shaping wood. With the saw alone, equipped with some regular blades and a jig or two, you can taper stock, make basic mouldings, cut coves and even cut pieces to match a pattern. Add a moulding head (a special blade with interchangeable profile cutters) and the possibilities are almost limitless. In fact, because of its tilting arbor, the table saw is capable of cutting profiles that no other machine can match.

■ *cutting tapers*

As you already know, the table saw excels at cutting straight lines, and a taper cut is a straight cut. So the only trick to making an accurate taper is holding the stock in the proper relationship to the blade. A number of taper jigs are on the market, and you can find plans for similar ones in other woodworking books. I've tried them and find that although they work, they are a lot more complicated than they have to be.

With these jigs, you have to worry about angles and the rise and run of the taper — too much math and too much thinking for my taste. Plus you have to buy or build the jig to begin with. I prefer to stick with a much simpler system that relies on drawing the taper you're after directly on your workpiece. Then, rather than using a specific tapering jig, I attach stop-blocks to a straight, flat length of 1×8 (or occasionally a piece of scrap plywood) that I keep near the saw for just such an occasion. This 1×8 carrier board is about 5' long, which accommodates almost any length of wood I am likely to need to cut. The stop-blocks hold the workpiece in the right position, and it is a simple matter to push the whole thing past the blade to make the cut. Even double tapers (where the workpiece tapers on opposite sides) are a snap. Just reset the stop-blocks for the second cut.

Start tapering by laying out the cut you want on your workpiece. Extend the ends of the line down the face or end of the piece.

Hold the workpiece in place with the layout line in line with the edge of the carrier board. Screw a long stop-block to the carrier board along the back edge of the workpiece. Double-check the workpiece's alignment with the edge, then screw a second stop-block at the trailing end of the work-piece to keep the piece from shifting.

Don't Give Your Saw a Wedgie

Be alert as you cut tapers. The offcut piece will often be a slender wedge. Sometimes these pieces drop away as they are cut free and jam between the blade and the throat plate. Keeping a splitter on the saw as you cut and using a throat plate that fits tightly to the blade will help prevent this. If it does occur, however, don't panic. Just carefully shut off the saw without letting go of the carrier board, unless it is completely clear of the blade.

Set the distance from the blade to the rip fence so it is equal to the width of the carrier board. If the workpiece is narrow like this table leg, screw some toggle clamps to the stop-blocks to help secure the workpiece to the carrier. Push the assembly past the blade to make the cut.

With the carrier system, even small pieces like this drawer pull can be cut safely. Here, the stop-blocks position a small drawer pull while a toggle clamp holds it securely in place. I like to keep my thumb on the piece, too, to make sure the clamp doesn't slip.

A Profile Library

Each time you design a new profile, keep a sample with any relevant notes written on the back side. After a while you will build up a library of potential profiles to refer to as you plan your next endeavor. The samples also make setting up your saw much easier as you can refer to them for the angles, kerf spacing and so on.

hot tip

■ *making mouldings*

Mouldings are to cabinets and furniture as icing is to a cake. They lend style to what would otherwise be a plain box. They also serve as a transition element between different surfaces and help disguise awkward or difficult-to-finish areas. While mouldings vary greatly in profile, there are few times when you actually see that profile. Usually mouldings are viewed as ribbons of line and shadow streaking across a surface or surrounding part of a cabinet such as a door. It is only when the moulding abuts another surface that the profile is truly evident.

This is not to say that all mouldings are interchangeable. But it is possible to create some very nice mouldings without resorting to expensive shaper cutters and router bits. By employing a combination of shallow saw kerfs, bevels, rabbets and dadoes, you can cut many simple mouldings on the table saw using only your regular blades and dado head. When you add the cove cut (discussed later in this chapter), the possibilities are almost limitless.

It is amazing how many profiles you can cut on a table saw with little more than a regular saw blade, dado head or moulding head. The examples shown here (from left to right) include (1) mirror frame; (2) window casing; (3) door casing; (4) cabinet stile (a vertical piece that bridges two cabinets); (5) picture frame; (6) mirror frame; and (7) door casing.

■ *cutting a picture frame moulding*

The following photos show an example of the steps to take to cut a simple but attractive picture frame moulding. Feel free to vary the dimensions to suit your own sense of aesthetics.

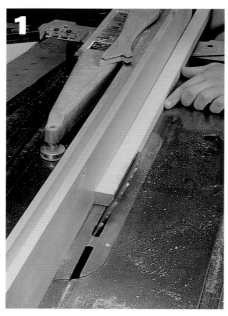

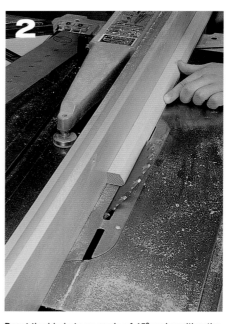

Start by cutting your stock to the dimensions needed. For this moulding use stock that is $^{13}/_{16}$"-wide by 1"-thick by the length needed for your picture. Tilt the blade to an angle of 60° and set the fence $^{11}/_{16}$" away from it. Make the first bevel cut.

Reset the blade to an angle of 45° and position the fence $^{3}/_{4}$" away from it. Make the second bevel cut.

Frame Profile

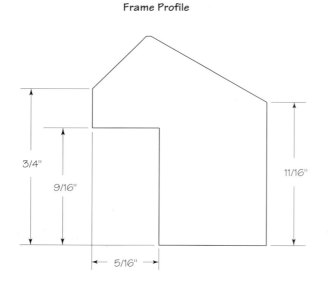

3/4"

9/16"

11/16"

5/16"

As a final cut, set up your dado head and rabbeting fence to cut a $^{5}/_{16}$" × $^{9}/_{16}$" rabbet. After a little sanding and some miter joints, you'll have a nice picture frame.

cutting coves

One of the most improbable operations you can do on a table saw is a cove cut. Coving uses the curve of the blade to create a rounded cut much like what you might expect from a router or shaper. The main difference is that the cove a table saw can make is much bigger than is possible with either the router or shaper. It can also occur in the center of a board, no matter how wide the board.

The trick to making a cove cut is to run the workpiece past the blade at an angle, rather than parallel to it as is normal. The blade height determines the depth of the cove while the angle of the coving fence (a shop-made jig) determines its width. Set up your coving fence at a slight angle to the blade and the resulting cove will be fairly narrow, such as one of the flutes in a fluted moulding. Increase the angle and the width of the cove grows.

Theoretically, on a 10" saw, you could cut a cove that is about 3" deep and about 9" wide if you set up your fence perpendi-

cular to the blade. It is also possible to make a half cove, such as you might see on the bevel of a raised panel.

The real key to successful coving is to take your time. Saw blades weren't really meant to cut this way, so you'll have to make the cove in a series of shallow passes, raising the blade slightly after each cut. Expect to do some serious scraping and sanding after making the cut; the surface a regular saw blade leaves is fairly coarse.

As for saw blades, you can cove with any blade. Before I obtained some more specialized tooling, I did most of my coving with a Freud 50-tooth combination blade. For a nicer finish you can also cut coves with a moulding head, such as the Magic Molder (discussed in "Using a Moulding Head," later in this chapter) equipped with bullnose cutters, or you can use a dedicated cove cutter (see "A Better Cove Cutter" later in this chapter). While these specialty cutters are somewhat pricey, they do a beautiful job of coving.

Cove jig hole detail

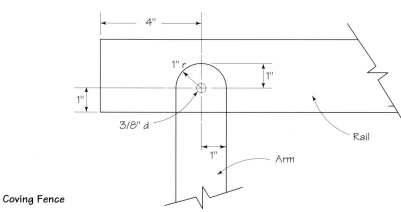

Coving Fence

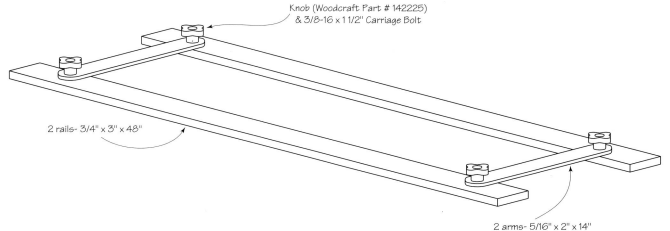

Knob (Woodcraft Part # 142225) & 3/8-16 x 1 1/2" Carriage Bolt

2 rails- 3/4" x 3" x 48"

2 arms- 5/16" x 2" x 14"

Start by laying out the cove you are after on the end of your workpiece. Don't worry too much about the shape of the curve. Just make sure the curve starts and ends where you want it to, and that it is the necessary depth. You should leave at least ⅛" of a flat on either side of the cove.

Set the distance between the parallel coving fences to match the width of the cove you laid out. Check at several points along the fences to make sure they are, in fact, parallel.

Set the blade height to match the cove depth. Position the fence on the saw table so the back fence just touches the blade where it emerges from the table on the outfeed side, and the front fence touches the blade where it dives beneath the table on the infeed side. Mark the fence positions on the table with a pencil.

A Better Cove Cutter

The one disadvantage of coving on the table saw is that the cut a regular saw blade produces is pretty rough. This translates to a lot of scraping and sanding to make the surface presentable. For one or two coves, in soft wood, this isn't so bad. But for much more than that, you'll start to wonder if there isn't a better way. Well, there is.

CMT has come out with a dedicated cove cutter. It is a heavy chunk of machined steel equipped with rounded carbide teeth. It comes as part of a set used to make raised-panel doors. The set includes both the cove cutter and some router bits for cutting the corner joinery. It is a pretty slick system. If you do a lot of coving, you will probably be able to recoup the cost of the cutter in abrasives alone.

Reset the space between the fences to match the overall width of the workpiece. Clamp the fences to the saw table, parallel to the layout lines you made earlier. (The lines in the photo were drawn with a grease pencil so they would show up in print.) The distance between the lines and the fences should match the width of the flats on either side of the cove. Remove the arms connecting the fences.

Lower the blade until it is only about $1/16$" above the table. Remove the pivot arms from the fences. Feed the workpiece between the fences and across the blade slowly and steadily. Use a push stick to keep your fingers away from the blade. Listen to the sound the saw makes; it should not sound much different than usual. If it starts to complain, slow down the feed or lower the blade slightly. Raise the blade slightly and make another pass. Continue to make shallow cuts in this manner until the full depth is reached.

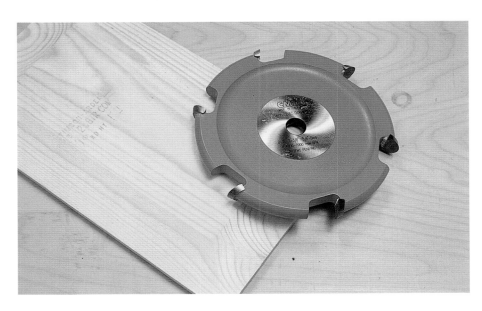

The cut produced by a dedicated cove cutter is much smoother than that produced by a regular saw blade. Using one of these cutters will save you a lot of time and sandpaper.

▮ *cutting half a cove*

When cutting coves for raised panels or box lids, you actually need to cut only half a cove. The setup for this cut is similar to that for a full cove; however the fence actually runs right over the blade rather than on either side.

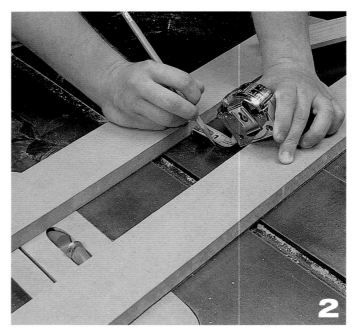

Set the blade height to match the cove depth. Position the coving fence as you would for a full-width cove. At two points, one on either side of the blade, measure halfway between the fences and mark the saw table.

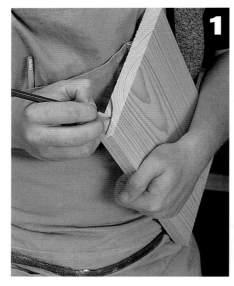

Lay out the cove you are after on the end of your stock. Again, the exact curve isn't critical as long as you have the right width and depth of the cut marked. Set the coving fence to double the width of the cove.

Lower the blade beneath the table. Align a straightedge with the halfway marks and clamp it to the table. The straightedge should cover the front half of the blade. Note: You will be cutting into the straightedge, so you may prefer to use a straight scrap rather than your coving fence.

Angled Coving

You can add a twist to your cove-cutting by tilting the arbor on the saw, as well as running the workpiece past the blade at an angle. Because the results are not nearly as easy to visualize as they are with the blade straight up and down, it is worth making a few sample pieces so you can begin to predict the final outcome.

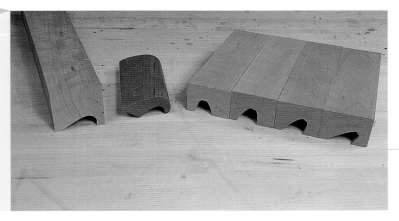

These cuts were made by running the pieces at an 8° angle to the blade. The blade angle was (from right to left) 45°, 60°, 75° and 90°. At the left is a drawer pull made with an angled cove cut and the piece the pull was cut from.

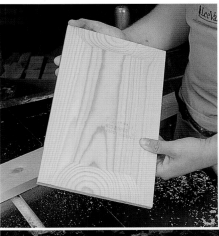

Raise the blade up until it just barely bites into the fence. Run your workpiece along the fence past the blade. Raise the blade up $1/16$" and make another pass. Continue in this manner until the cove is cut to the proper depth. If you are coving all four edges of a piece, make the cuts across the grain first. This way any tear-out will be cut away when you make the long-grain cuts.

4

■ *using a moulding head*

A moulding head is another accessory you can purchase to expand the capabilities of your saw. You can cut various moulding profiles, as well as a number of joints, such as the tongue-and-groove and locking miter. Both Sears and Delta have sold moulding heads for years. These devices consist of a steel hub with slots and locking screws that hold interchangeable steel profile knives. These moulding heads generally come with six sets of knives. More knife sets are available individually.

The steel knives in these moulding heads do an acceptable job of cutting profiles in solid wood, though they become dull much faster than a carbide blade will. This is particularly true if you use them to cut MDF (medium-density fiberboard) or other abrasive, manufactured sheet stock. The quality of the cut is a little rougher than you would expect from a sharp router bit or shaper cutter.

Recently, a company called LRH Enterprises came out with an updated version of the traditional moulding head called a Magic Molder. This tool features an anodized aluminum hub that accepts what they call detail plugs. A detail plug is similar to a moulding knife except that the cutter itself is made of carbide. The plugs are used in pairs and lock securely and precisely in the hub. They make use of the latest antikickback technology that limits the size of the bite the plug can take. This practically eliminates the chance of kickback and means you can use the Magic Molder on a saw with a smaller motor (because the cutter isn't taking too big a bite, it doesn't need a lot of power to cut). LRH makes a wide variety of profiles, and they will make custom plugs to your specifications.

The traditional steel moulding head is a good investment if cutting profiles is something you do only on an occasional basis. When assembled, the cutter is about 6" in diameter and can make a maximum cut about ¾" deep. The choice of cutters is somewhat limited.

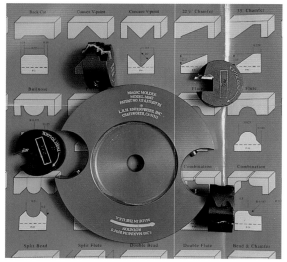

For a little more money (OK, for a lot more money), the Magic Molder turns your saw into a moulding machine that also happens to be a table saw. The carbide-tipped cutters leave a crisp, clean surface and are available in a wide variety of profiles. If you use a lot of mouldings in your work, this setup is well worth the added investment.

Sanding on the Table Saw

By replacing the blade on your saw with a 10" steel disc with a piece of abrasive paper adhered, you can make yourself a precise disc sander for a fraction of the cost of a stand-alone machine. These discs are flat on one side and slightly tapered (thicker in the middle, thinner at the rim) on the other. The flat side works quite well for general-purpose sanding. You should sand only on the front portion of the disc – the part that is turning toward the table. If you try to sand on the rear part of the disc, the abrasive will try to pick your stock up and throw it across the room.

The tapered side allows you to use the disc as a sort of jointer. To do this, tilt the arbor on the saw over slightly so the tapered surface is at 90° to the table when measured directly above the arbor. Then run your stock along between the fence and the disc. Because of the taper, the disc will be in contact with the piece only along a line directly above the arbor. If you set the angle correctly, the abrasive will just kiss the edge of your stock lightly, cleaning it up beautifully. The straightness of the sanded edge is determined by the straightness of the edge that is running against the fence.

To set up a moulding head, mount the tool on your saw. Both styles have a spacer to position the head the proper distance away from the flange on the arbor. Use a throat plate with a wide opening, such as the one you use for dadoing, or make a throat plate specifically for use with the moulding head as described in "Looking After Blades" in chapter five, "Tuning Up Your Saw." Draw the profile on your stock and use this as a guide to set the fence.

With either moulding head, you are not obligated to use the entire profile. By burying part of the cutter within a fence, you can use whatever portion of the cutter you need. The folks at LRH make a fence for this purpose that they sell as a Magic Molder accessory, but you can also use a rabbeting fence (described in "Cutting Rabbets" in chapter two, "Joinery") to do the same thing.

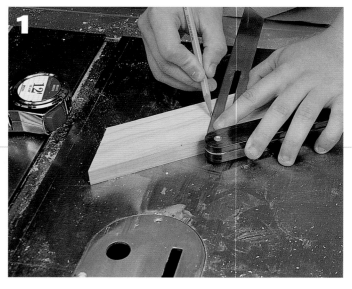

1

Cut the featherboard to the specified width and length, and cut one end at about a 50° angle. Draw an angled line across the piece 3½" from the angled end.

■ *featherboards*

Featherboards are a great aid when it comes to making mouldings. Actually, they can be useful for a lot of table saw operations, especially those involving thin or narrow pieces. They can be positioned to help keep pieces down on the table and against the rip fence.

There are two different featherboards featured in "Eliminating Chatter," below. The first is a double featherboard, which features two featherboards mounted on an MDF backer board. The backer board gets screwed to the rip fence, and the two featherboards can be adjusted to exert pressure on the workpiece.

The second featherboard is a commercial model that I like a lot. It is attached to a short aluminum bar that rides in the miter gauge slot. When you tighten the knob, the bar expands, locking the featherboard in place. This type of featherboard can be positioned to hold pieces against the rip fence. It is available from a number of woodworking suppliers, including Woodcraft.

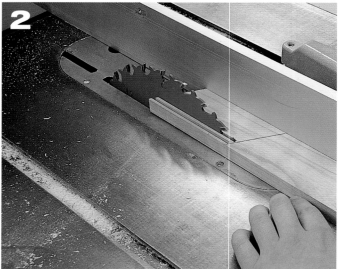

2

Set the fence to make a cut ¼" narrower than the overall width of the piece. Cut in as far as the line, then carefully back the piece out of the cut. Move the fence over ¼" and repeat. Continue in this manner until you have cut all the feathers. On the last cut, the fence should be only ⅛" from the blade.

Eliminating Chatter

For the cleanest possible cut, you want to run the stock past the moulding head as smoothly and steadily as possible. Setting up featherboards to keep the stock down on the table and pressed against the fence will help keep the workpiece from chattering as it is cut. You can easily make featherboards yourself as above.

hot tip

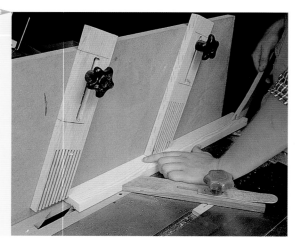

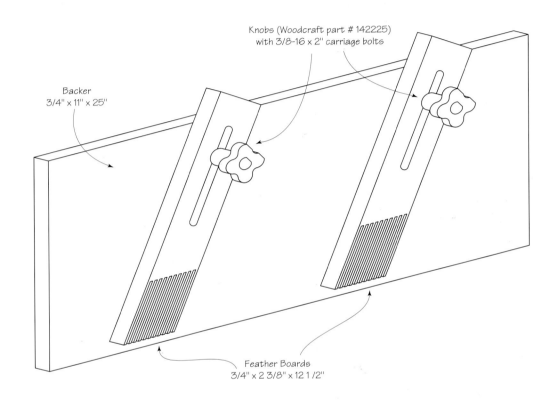

Knobs (Woodcraft part # 142225)
with 3/8-16 x 2" carriage bolts

Backer
3/4" x 11" x 25"

Feather Boards
3/4" x 2 3/8" x 12 1/2"

Groove and Hole Details

8 1/8"

11"

1 3/4"

3/8" Wide
Groove

1 9/16"

1"

5 1/8"

◼ *cutting to a pattern*

Cutting a number of pieces to the same size is a straightforward job if the pieces are rectangular. But when the end result is not a nice simple shape, this pattern-sawing trick is worth knowing. It is particularly useful if the shape is one you will revisit from time to time. I used to work in a shop where we had to produce pentagonal pieces, several dozen at a time, every other month or so. After the first couple of orders where we spent half an hour or so making a fresh layout and working out the miter gauge settings, we made a pattern and hung it on the wall. Then it was a simple matter to set up the saw with the pattern-cutting fence and to knock out the order in less time than it took to draw an accurate pentagon.

The key to cutting to a pattern is the pattern-cutting fence. This fence attaches to the rip fence and hangs over the blade. The edge of the fence should be set flush with the outside edge of the blade. The pattern-cutting fence serves as a guide in much the same way the bearing on a router bit does. The pattern is attached to the workpiece. Then the pattern rides along the pattern-cutting fence, and the workpiece is trimmed to shape. Make sure each side of your patterns is long enough to provide good contact with the fence. If the pattern doesn't feel stable on one side, leave that cut for last, and set it up with a stop-block on the miter gauge.

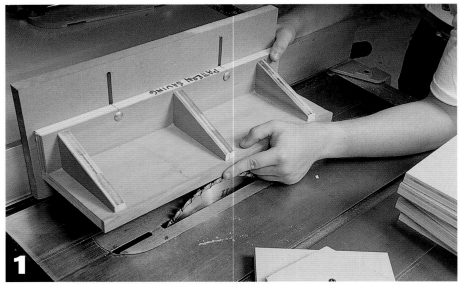

Attach the pattern-cutting fence to the rip fence. Set the height of the pattern-cutting fence so it is about $1/4"$ higher than the thickness of your workpieces. Adjust the rip fence so the edge of the pattern-cutting fence is flush with the outside of the saw blade.

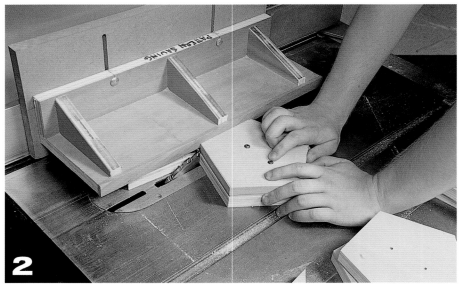

Make your template from $1/2"$ MDF. Attach it to the workpiece with nails, screws or double-sided tape. Make sure there is enough room between the blade and the fence for the offcut. If necessary, trim the pieces closer to the final size. To make the cut, run the pattern along the pattern-cutting fence.

Clearing the Offcuts

When you are pattern cutting, the offcut pieces can collect under the pattern-cutting fence, creating a nuisance, if not a kickback hazard. A quick blast of compressed air after every two or three cuts will keep the area clear without your having to shut down the saw or risk poking under the fence with a stick or other item that could get caught in the blade.

Pattern-Cutting Fence

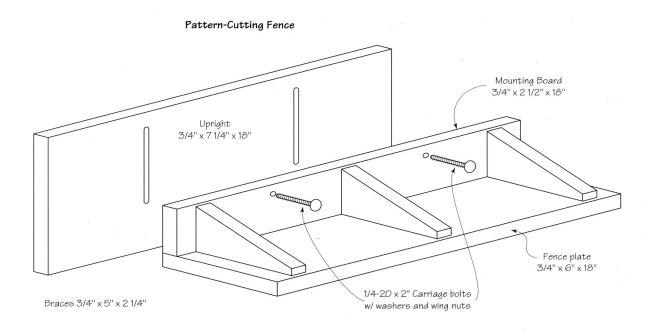

Upright
3/4" x 7 1/4" x 18"

Mounting Board
3/4" x 2 1/2" x 18"

Fence plate
3/4" x 6" x 18"

1/4-20 x 2" Carriage bolts
w/ washers and wing nuts

Braces 3/4" x 5" x 2 1/4"

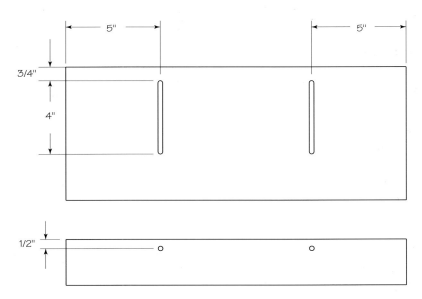

Groove and Hole Details

■ *kerf bending*

Kerf bending is perhaps the simplest method of bending wood. It is not necessarily the best or the strongest, but it is definitely quick and easy. And in many situations it is perfectly adequate for the job. Kerf bending involves cutting a series of kerfs across the piece you want to bend, leaving a thin ($1/4$" or less, depending on how much bend you need), flexible strip of wood on one side. The kerfs should be evenly spaced so the bend will be consistent. Obviously, the kerfed side of the piece is not going to be particularly presentable when you are finished. Nor will the edges look very good, so you will need to plan how to deal with these issues in your design. You'll also need to add support to the piece after it is bent to help hold the curve and to lend strength to the piece. After all, it has only $1/8$" or so of wood holding the whole thing together.

Once the piece has been kerfed, you can bend it to either a concave or convex shape. The closer together the kerfs are, and the deeper they are cut, the tighter a bend you can get out of a piece of wood. Some woods such as oak and ash bend a lot more readily than wood such as cherry and mahogany.

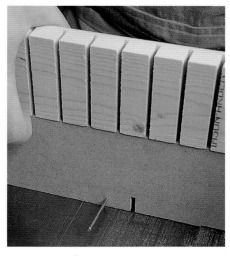

Cutting the kerfs is similar to cutting the pins in a box joint (described in "Cutting Box Joints," in chapter two, "Joinery") where each subsequent kerf uses the previous kerf as a reference. However, rather than building an elaborate jig, I usually just drive a finish nail into an extension fence attached to the miter gauge.

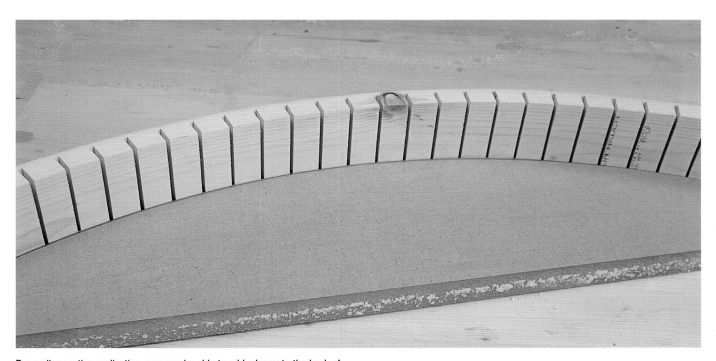

Depending on the application, you may be able to add a brace to the back of the piece for support. I have seen kerf bent mouldings that are reinforced by the wall or the piece they are attached to.

cutting sheet stock

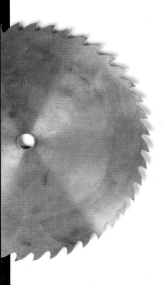

SHEET STOCK, PLYWOOD, MDF, melamine board, etc., is a mainstay of many cabinet shops and a necessary evil in many others. It is the rare woodworker who doesn't use at least a sheet or two sometime in the course of a year, if only for making a jig or the occasional utility cabinet. Depending on how and where your shop is set up, dealing with 4×8 sheet stock can be no big deal, or it can be a real headache.

My first shop was in the basement of a narrow row house in Allentown, Pennsylvania. I had a pretty complete range of equipment down there — table saw, band saw, jointer, planer and drill press. All of it was carried down one piece at a time and reassembled on the spot. I can still remember the way the stairs groaned under the weight of the jointer as we bumped it down, strapped to a dolly.

I could rip boards that were about 5' long in one pass; longer ones I had to flip end for end to avoid running into the furnace. Even if I could have carried full sheets of plywood down to the basement, there is no way I could have cut them up. Heck, there was hardly enough room to turn around down there. Still, I built quite a few cabinets and other projects in that shop, using a wide range of different sheet stock. The secret was to de-

velop techniques that allowed me to work around the limitations of my space. The main trick I used was to cut the material roughly to size before carrying it down the stairs. Sometimes I did this in the backyard with a hand-held circular saw; other times I would take advantage of the folks at the home center where I purchased the material and have them cut it for me. If you go this route, you have to have a bit of a sense of humor, because precision measurement isn't something home centers guarantee.

I have a lot more space in my current shop. In fact, when I designed the building, the table saw was the first piece of equipment I placed, and I left 10' in front of and behind the machine with the idea that I would be handling a fair amount of sheet stock. I also left about 6' to the left of the blade with sheet stock in mind. In hindsight, I wish I had at least 8' to the left of the blade, but 6' isn't bad.

Still, even with the necessary space, dealing with full sheets of plywood isn't exactly easy, especially if you work alone. With that in mind, this chapter has a number of strategies for working with sheet stock, from cutting it down into manageable pieces, to working around the limitations imposed by a saw with a limited rip capacity to avoiding tear-out.

■ setting up to handle sheet stock

Table saws come in varying degrees of readiness to handle cutting sheet stock. Some, like the big European-style saws with an integral sliding table, require little added preparation. Others, such as the typical contractor's saw, require quite a bit more. In between are the cabinet saws, which sport an extended table to the right of the blade and a rip fence with a 50"–52" capacity.

At the very least, you need some kind of outfeed support to hold the pieces up as they are cut. In my shop, positioned immediately behind the saw, I have an outfeed table that is set up all the time. Its top is an old kitchen counter, and it stands on a base cobbled together from scraps of various projects. Eventually I plan to upgrade the base with some cabinets to add a little sorely needed storage space. I use this table all the time for cutting both solid wood and sheet stock. However, if your space is tight, you may not want to commit the space to such a permanent landmark. In this case, a roller stand or two, or a pair of sawhorses made to match the height of your saw will do the trick.

Another handy device to have is an outrigger to support stock that is hanging out over the left side of the saw. (Those of you lucky folks with a sliding table can ignore this one.) I started out with a single sawhorse made to match the height of my saw table. I have gradually modified the

My outfeed table is a recycled kitchen countertop. The plastic laminate surface works well for this purpose as pieces slide well across it. The counter also doubles as an assembly table. Here, too, the laminate surface is an advantage: Spilled glue just pops right off. I keep the table about 1' away from the saw. This provides clearance for the miter gauge bar, and allows me to slide cutoffs into a scrap bin that waits right behind the saw.

design and now use a pair of horses that I bolt together end to end. This creates a support beam that runs from about 3' in front of the saw to about 4' past the blade.

The final device is an infeed table. While this one isn't as critical as an outfeed table, it does make life a lot easier. My infeed table is an addition to a mobile materials cart I built, based loosely on a design Jim Tolpin presented in his book *Working at Woodworking* (Taunton Press, 1991). I use the cart to move project parts around the shop as they progress from machine to machine for various opera-

tions. To convert the cart into an infeed table for sheet stock, I add a grid of 2×4s to increase the size of the tabletop. The bottom of the cart is weighted with sand to keep the cart from tipping over. When I get a load of plywood, I wheel the cart over to the door and take the plywood from the back of my truck and stack it right on the grid. Then I wheel the cart over to the saw and feed the pieces right off the top of the stack. Locking casters on the cart keep it from shifting as I slide the pieces off of it. When the grid is not needed, the pieces come off and are stored.

By clamping a pair of sawhorses together, I create a long outrigger that helps support offcut pieces of sheet stock until I can clear the other side of the piece from the saw. When you set up the outrigger, angle it slightly toward the rear of the fence. This will help keep the stock riding against the fence as you cut.

With its auxiliary rails in place, my materials cart can handle up to eight sheets of ¾" material and present it at a good height for sawing. When the grid is not in use, it quickly detaches, leaving the cart free to carry other stock.

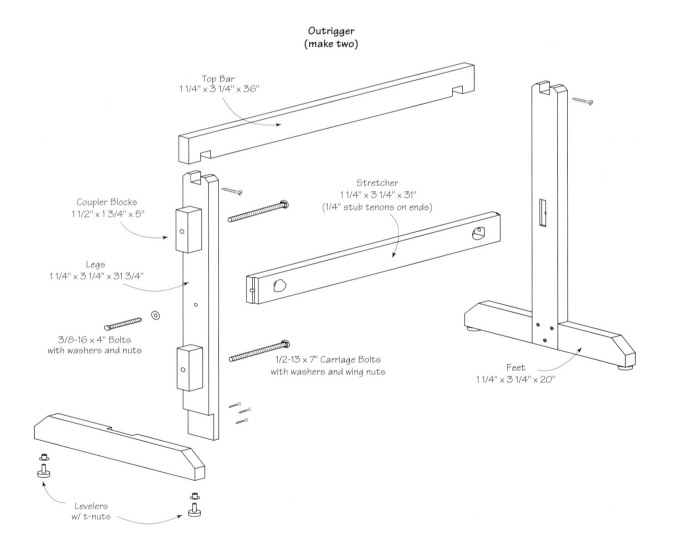

Outrigger
(make two)

Top Bar
1 1/4" x 3 1/4" x 36"

Coupler Blocks
1 1/2" x 1 3/4" x 5"

Legs
1 1/4" x 3 1/4" x 31 3/4"

3/8-16 x 4" Bolts
with washers and nuts

1/2-13 x 7" Carriage Bolts
with washers and wing nuts

Stretcher
1 1/4" x 3 1/4" x 31"
(1/4" stub tenons on ends)

Feet
1 1/4" x 3 1/4" x 20"

Levelers
w/ t-nuts

MATERIALS LIST inches

REFERENCE	QUANTITY	PART	STOCK	THICKNESS	WIDTH	LENGTH
A	4	wide legs	pine 1×5 plywood	$3/4$	$4^1/4$	$31^3/4$
B	4	narrow legs	pine 1×5 plywood	$3/4$	$3^1/2$	$31^3/4$
C	2	long aprons	pine 1×5 plywood	$3/4$	$4^1/2$	$49^1/2$
D	2	short aprons	pine 1×5 plywood	$3/4$	$4^1/2$	41
E	4	corner braces	pine 1×5 plywood	$3/4$	$4^1/2$	$8^1/4$
F	4	foot blocks	pine 1×5 plywood	$1^3/4$	$1^3/4$	5
G	1	top	pine 1×5 plywood	$3/4$	44	54
H	3	long stiffeners	pine 1×4 plywood	$3/4$	3	48
J	2	short stiffeners	pine 1×4 plywood	$3/4$	3	44
K	1	plastic laminate			48	60

HARDWARE

Assorted screws

4 – $3/8$" T-nuts

4 – $3/8$" × $1^1/2$" leveler feet

MATERIALS LIST millimeters

REFERENCE	QUANTITY	PART	STOCK	THICKNESS	WIDTH	LENGTH
A	4	wide legs	pine 1×5 plywood	19	108	806
B	4	narrow legs	pine 1×5 plywood	19	89	806
C	2	long aprons	pine 1×5 plywood	19	115	1258
D	2	short aprons	pine 1×5 plywood	19	115	1041
E	4	corner braces	pine 1×5 plywood	19	115	209
F	4	foot blocks	pine 1×5 plywood	45	45	127
G	1	top	pine 1×5 plywood	19	1118	1372
H	3	long stiffeners	pine 1×4 plywood	19	76	1219
J	2	short stiffeners	pine 1×4 plywood	19	76	1118
K	1	plastic laminate			1219	1524

HARDWARE

Assorted screws

4 – 10mm T-nuts

4 – 10mm × 38mm leveler feet

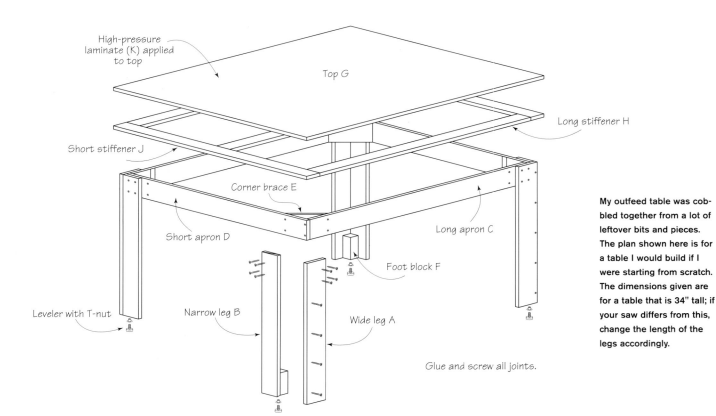

High-pressure laminate (K) applied to top

Top G

Long stiffener H

Short stiffener J

Corner brace E

Short apron D

Long apron C

Foot block F

Leveler with T-nut

Narrow leg B

Wide leg A

Glue and screw all joints.

My outfeed table was cobbled together from a lot of leftover bits and pieces. The plan shown here is for a table I would build if I were starting from scratch. The dimensions given are for a table that is 34" tall; if your saw differs from this, change the length of the legs accordingly.

REFERENCE	QUANTITY	PART	STOCK	THICKNESS	WIDTH	LENGTH
A	4	wide legs	pine 1×4	3/4	3 1/2	23 1/4
B	4	narrow legs	pine 1×4	3/4	2 3/4	23 1/4
C	2	long aprons	pine 1×4	3/4	3 1/2	36
D	3	short aprons	pine 1×4	3/4	3 1/2	16 1/4
E	2	long stretchers	pine 1×4	3/4	3 1/2	36
F	2	short stretchers	pine 1×4	3/4	3 1/2	17 1/8
G	2	shelf/bottom	pine 1×4	1/2	17 1/8	35 3/8
H	1	support	pine 1×4	3/4	2 1/2	16 1/4
J	4	caster pads	pine 1×4	3/4	3 1/2	3 1/2
K	2	runners	hardwood	1	3 1/2	72
L	2	arms	hardwood	1	3 1/2	40
M	1	top	plywood	3/4	21 3/4	40 1/2

MATERIALS LIST **millimeters**

HARDWARE

Assorted screws

4 Heavy-duty castors

REFERENCE	QUANTITY	PART	STOCK	THICKNESS	WIDTH	LENGTH
A	4	wide legs	pine 1×4	19	89	590
B	4	narrow legs	pine 1×4	19	70	590
C	2	long aprons	pine 1×4	19	89	914
D	3	short aprons	pine 1×4	19	89	412
E	2	long stretchers	pine 1×4	19	89	914
F	2	short stretchers	pine 1×4	19	89	435
G	2	shelf/bottom	pine 1×4	13	435	899
H	1	support	pine 1×4	19	64	412
J	4	caster pads	pine 1×4	19	89	89
K	2	runners	hardwood	25	89	1829
L	2	arms	hardwood	25	89	1016
M	1	top	plywood	19	552	1029

Of all the changes I made to my shop in the course of writing this book, I think this cart is the best. Before, when I cut stock on the table saw, I'd have the pieces stacked everywhere, cluttering every available surface. Now when I work I have a nice, neat stack on my cart ready to be wheeled over to the next machine or operation. This was well worth the time and materials it took. The one feature you can't see from the photos is hidden under the shelf. The entire bottom unit of the cart is filled with about 100 pounds of sand. This added weight helps keep the cart from vibrating too much as I roll it across the shop floor. And it also keeps the cart from tipping under a load of plywood. As you build the shelf, dump in the sand before gluing on the top.

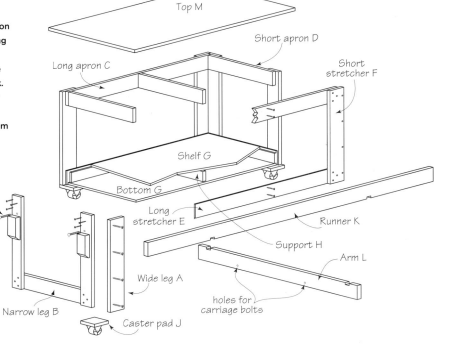

Top M

Short apron D

Long apron C

Short stretcher F

Shelf G

Bottom G

Long stretcher E

Runner K

Support H

Arm L

Carriage bolts 3/8-16 x 2" with washers and wing nuts

Wide leg A

holes for carriage bolts

Narrow leg B

Caster pad J

cutting sheet stock

In general, most cuts in sheet stock are made against the rip fence because the pieces being cut have nice long edges. With this in mind, if a piece is particularly narrow and it looks like the miter gauge would be a better choice, use the miter gauge. The terms ripping and crosscutting are relative. The grain in plywood runs in both directions, and the grain in MDF and particleboard is pretty much unidirectional, so I think of ripping and crosscutting in terms of the grain on the face veneer. This holds true for the length and width of the pieces, too. The length is measured with the grain of the face veneer, and the width is measured across it, even if the piece is wider than it is long. With stock that doesn't have a face veneer, the long dimension is its length.

As I cut up sheet stock, my ultimate goal is to eliminate all the factory edges on every piece. This is not to say that the factory edges don't have their uses; they make great references from which to work. However, I find that by the time the sheets show up in my shop, the factory edges have been bruised and banged enough that they are not really suitable for edge-banding or joinery, so I cut them after making use of their straight edges. This usually means I will cut a piece several times to get it to the right dimension.

The first cut brings the piece roughly to size, within ½" to 1" of final size. Often this first cut is made in a large piece of sheet stock and may not be as clean an edge as I would prefer. It is straight

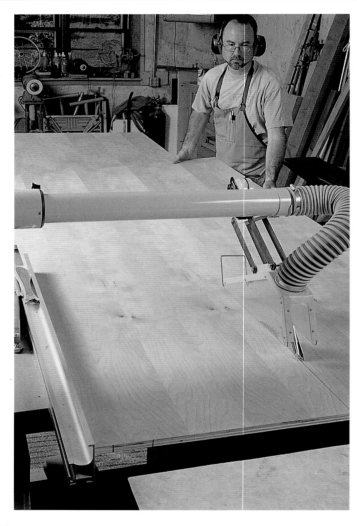

Often the first cut I make in a piece of sheet stock is to cut it in half lengthwise. While a full sheet is not the easiest thing to handle solo, I find I can make this cut without too much difficulty. Stand at the left rear corner of the sheet. Here, you can apply pressure both forward and against the fence as you push the piece past the blade. At the end of the cut push both pieces past the blade onto your outfeed table or rollers.

enough, however, to use as a reference. I turn this piece around and run the freshly cut edge against the fence, cutting off the factory edge but still leaving the piece oversize. When I have all the pieces ready to be cut to final size, I set the fence and trim away the edge created by the initial cut. It sounds like a lot of work, but the results are panels with edges that are as crisp and clean as possible.

A Cutting Guide

If your space, your saw or your strength (or any combination thereof) is limited, you'll find it easier to cut sheet stock into smaller pieces before pushing it across the table saw. Lay out the cuts with a chalk line. I leave about 1" extra to account for the tear-out that is likely to occur. Make the cuts with a circular saw or a saber saw.

If you choose to use a circular saw, you can make a cutting guide that makes getting a straight cut easy. The guide is simple to make. Start with a piece of 1/4" plywood that is about 3" wider than base of your saw. Attach this to a 3"-wide piece of 3/4" material. The 3/4" piece will serve as a fence to guide your saw.

After the pieces are fastened together, run your saw down the jig. This will trim the 1/4" piece to match the exact dimension of your saw between the edge of the saw's base and the blade. When you attach the guide to the sheet you want to cut, align the edge of the guide with your cut line.

If the first cut I have to make in a sheet is a crosscut, I'll cut the piece roughly to size with a circular saw. (See "A Cutting Guide," above.) I am not comfortable crosscutting an entire sheet on the table saw by myself. Once the pieces are a more manageable size, run them against the fence to trim away the rough edge left by the circular saw.

This cutting guide is fast to set up. Simply clamp it to the stock with the edge of the 1/4" plywood aligned with the cut line. I have two of these jigs. One is 52" wide for cutting across full sheets; the other is 96" long for cutting the length of full sheets.

■ *working around a limited rip capacity*

Even if you have a big shop, you can still be stuck when it comes time to cut up sheet stock if your saw has a limited rip capacity. On many contractor-style saws (and even some cabinet saws), the maximum distance the fence can be set to the right of the blade is between 25" and 30". This works fine if you have to cut a piece in half lengthwise, but if you need pieces that are 48" long, you have a problem.

The answer is to skip using the rip fence entirely. In fact, if the piece you're cutting is big enough, you may need to remove the fence from the saw. Instead of the fence, attach a straightedge to your workpiece and guide this along the edge of the saw table. This takes a little more effort than simply setting the fence to the right measurement, but it gives you the capability to accurately cut pieces that you could not cut otherwise.

Make the straightedge from a scrap of plywood or MDF that is about 4" wide and about 2' longer than the length of the cut you intend to make. If you decide you like this technique, keep a 4' and a 6' straightedge on hand and you'll be ready for almost any cut you'll need to make.

Note: For this series of photos, I am cutting a relatively small piece of material, because it's easier to show the process with a smaller piece of stock. I could have calculated what the waste would be and set the fence for that, less the thickness of the saw blade. That would yield the same result as the technique shown in the photos.

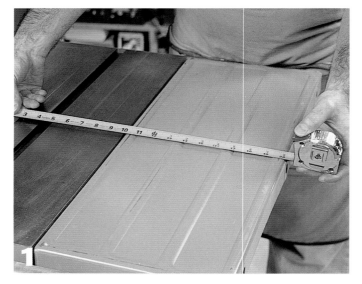

Measure from the left side of the blade to the edge of the saw table. Record this measurement. Check to make sure nothing will get in the way as you run a guide along the table's edge. On some saws the bars that hold the fence overlap the edge of the table.

Lay out the cut line on your stock. From this line, lay out a second line that is offset from the first by a distance equal to the distance from the blade to the edge of the table. I've made this line dark for the photo. Otherwise there is no need to do so; you'll just have to sand it away later.

However, cutting a small strip off a large piece can be awkward, and downright dangerous if done wrong. While involving a lengthier setup, guiding along the edge of the saw table is a lot safer and yields a much nicer cut.

Clamp a straightedge along the second layout line. Make sure the clamps are on the side of the straightedge, away from the cut line. The straightedge should extend beyond the edges of your stock by at least 12" on either side. Be careful not to mar the surface of the stock with the clamps.

Turn the assembly over and rest it on the edge of the saw table. Start the saw and push the piece through the cut, guiding the straightedge along the edge of the saw table.

Gaining Space

Several years ago, my parents asked me to build them a set of bookcases to go on either side of a new gas fireplace they were having installed. At the time, I was still working out of my small row-house shop, so I opted to use my father's shop. It, too, is in the basement, which makes cutting sheet stock a challenge. Rather than put up with this throughout the project, we relocated his table saw to the garage for a few weekends. This temporary change of venue made a big difference as we cut our way through a stack of cherry plywood.

hot tip

reducing tear-out

Tear-out, that slight (or major) splintering you experience when crosscutting a piece of material, is a nuisance when cutting solid stock. It means extra sanding and scraping, as well as potentially altering the profile of the moulding. These are minor woes compared to tear-out on a piece of sheet stock. With veneer, tear-out is practically fatal. What is worse, veneered stock tends to tear out if you look at it wrong. In reading about some blade tests in various magazines while researching this book, I found that often the most difficult material to crosscut (and groove) cleanly is birch veneer plywood. This pretty much matches my personal experience, although I will add that cutting melamine board, which is particleboard that comes prelaminated with a very thin layer of plastic laminate, runs a close second.

Here are a few strategies you can try to help eliminate or at least reduce the problem. First, use sharp, clean blades. I get out the blades I'll be using and take a good look at them at the start of a major project. I'll clean them at the very least. (See "Looking After Blades" in chapter five, "Tuning Up Your Saw.") Then I'll make a test cut in a scrap of birch plywood. If the blade tears out a lot, I send it out to be sharpened. (Hopefully I'll have remembered to have had my spare blade sharpened in the meantime.) Second, equip your saw with a zero-clearance throat plate. (See "Making Throat Plates" in chapter five, "Tuning Up Your Saw.") Third, for critical cuts, make a scoring cut first, before cutting all the way through the stock. And finally, apply a strip of masking tape along the cut line on the underside of the piece.

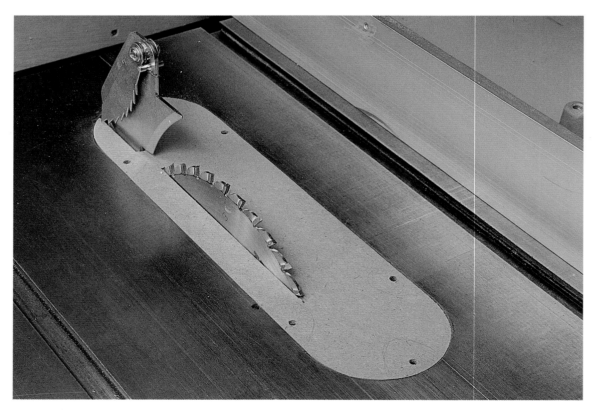

The typical throat plate leaves a gap at least 1/8" wide around the blade. This leaves the fragile veneer fibers unsupported as they are cut. With a fresh zero-clearance insert, there is no appreciable gap, so the veneer fibers are supported up to the point where the blade shears them off. This can make a big difference in how cleanly a blade cuts.

Preventing Tear-Out When Moulding

When cutting all four edges of a piece — rabbeting a panel to fit in a frame, or shaping the edges of a cutting board, for example — make the cuts across the grain first. Then make the long-grain cuts. This way, any tear-out along the trailing edge of the piece will be cut off when you make long-grain cuts.

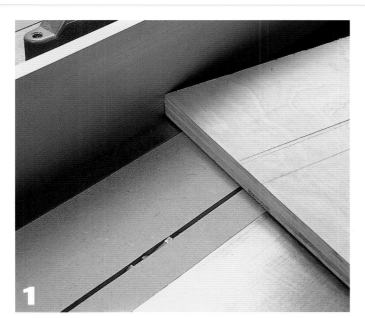

Many of the large commercial table saws include a scoring blade. This is a small-diameter saw blade that sits several inches in front of the main blade and spins in the opposite direction. This blade is set just above the table and scores the veneer before the main blade makes the cut. You can simulate this action by setting your saw blade for a shallow cut ($1/32$" $+/-$) and running each piece past before making the actual cut.

You can also apply a strip of masking tape along the underside of the cut line. Most tear-out occurs on the underside of a piece, so the tape will help support those fibers. You do run the risk, however, that the tape will lift the fibers as you remove it. Try it on a test piece first.

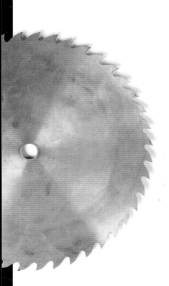

tuning up your saw

NO MATTER WHAT KIND OF SAW YOU own, it will perform better if you spend a little time, periodically, tuning it up. How often you do this depends a lot on how much you use your saw. I usually budget a day at the beginning of each major project, or before each class, to get the shop into tip-top condition.

This involves a thorough cleanup — blowing the dust out of everything, emptying the scrap bin, sweeping up and putting things away as well as tuning up all the equipment. As I move from one machine to the next I check the various alignments, lubricate the moving parts and sharpen or replace dull blades and cutters. I like to do this about a week before launching into the actual project if I have the luxury of time. This way I can send out any blades that need to be sharpened and bask in the simple pleasure of having a clean shop for a few days. By the time the blades are ready, I'm ready to get to work. Somehow it rarely works out this way, but when it does, it's a great feeling.

■ adjusting the table saw

A major part of getting a table saw to perform at its very best is to get all of the pieces into alignment with each other. This alignment centers on the blade. Check to make sure the blade itself is square to the table, then check that the miter gauge slots are parallel to the blade and the rip fence locks down parallel to the slots. If the saw is new to you (or if you've never checked), you may also want to check to see if the table extensions (the wings on either side of the main table) are aligned with the main table, and that the whole surface is flat. Make sure the saw is unplugged while you work on it.

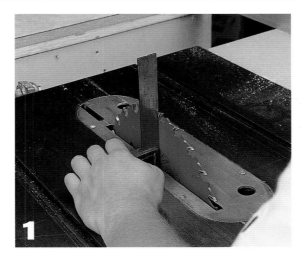

Start by checking to make sure that the blade is actually square to the table. There is a set screw that controls this on the curved rack that tilts the arbor. If necessary, tilt the blade over so you can access this screw. Loosen or tighten the set screw as needed so the blade stops exactly at 90° when it is tilted upright. Many times, the only adjustment necessary is to clean away the sawdust that has built up against the stop under the table.

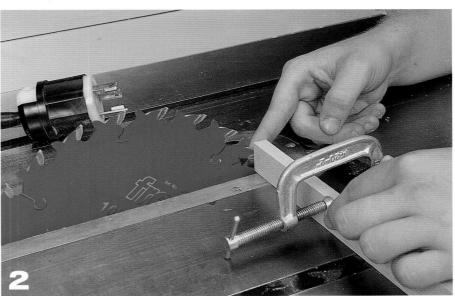

Next, check to see if the miter gauge slots are parallel to the blade. Choose a tooth on the blade and mark it with a marker. Clamp a scrap (I use a piece of maple, $\frac{1}{4}$" × 1" × 12") to your miter gauge so that the end of the wood barely kisses the marked tooth when the tooth is near the table toward the front of the saw.

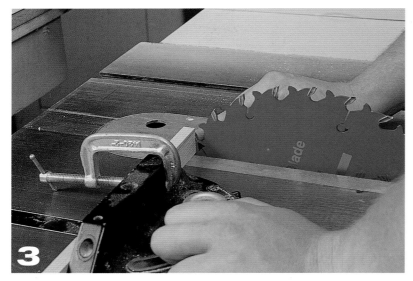

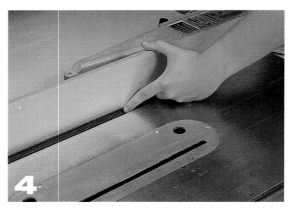

When you have the slots properly adjusted, check to make sure your fence locks down parallel to them. Align the fence with the edge of one slot and check with your finger to make sure the fence follows the slot along its entire length. Consult your owner's manual to see how to adjust the fence if necessary.

Slide the miter gauge and spin the blade toward the rear of the table. Check to see if the stick still just barely kisses the marked tooth. If so, then the slots are parallel to the blade; if not, you'll have to adjust. On a cabinet saw, loosen the bolts that hold the table to the base and shift the table slightly. On a contractor's saw, loosen the bolts that hold the arbor assembly to the under-side of the table and shift the arbor slightly. Keep the bolts rela-tively snug so the act of tightening them doesn't shift things out of position.

Next, check to make sure the extension wings are level with the main table by running your finger along the seams between them. If necessary, loosen the mounting bolts and raise or lower the wing. Also check with a straightedge to be sure the entire surface is flat. If the wings are made of stamped steel, you can usually bend them into alignment. If the wings are cast iron, loosen the mounting bolts and insert metal shims (cut from a clean soda can) in between the pieces as needed.

As a final step, tilt the blade all the way over and check to see if the 45° stop is set properly. This is a set screw similar to the one used to stop the blade at 90°.

The Brush Off

If you cut a lot of resinous woods such as pine, the underside parts of your saw can end up coated with a sticky film of dust and pitch. This yuck will quickly make moving the blade a real chore. I use a brass-bristled wire brush to remove this buildup, followed by an application of paraffin wax that restores mobility.

■ lubricating a table saw

The motor and arbor bearings on modern saws are sealed and do not require added lubrication. If you have an older saw, however, check to see if it has oil or grease fittings. If so, give them a shot of grease or light machine oil a couple of times a year. The parts that are worth lubricating on all saws are the trunnions and gears that raise and lower the blade and allow it to tilt. You'll also find your saw is a lot more pleasant to work with if you wax and buff the table as well as the rail(s) that the rip fence rides on. Not only will the wax make the table more slippery, but it will also help keep it from rusting. Note: The photos of the trunnions were shot with the saw turned upside down. There is no need for you to turn your saw over; this was the best way for me to get the photo.

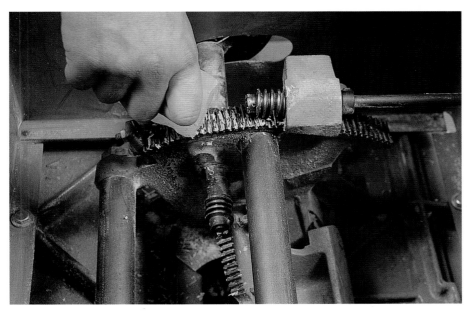

To keep the tilt and blade height mechanisms working freely, keep the gears clean and lubricated. Rather than grease or oil, use a dry lubricant that won't attract dust. (Imagine that, dust in a woodshop!) My preferred lubricant for this application is paraffin wax (available at most supermarkets near the canning supplies). Simply scrape the wax over the gears and other surfaces, then crank the blade up and down and tilt it a few times.

One of the most frequent tune-ups I perform is to wax and buff the saw table. It is amazing to me how much of a difference a coat of wax can make when you are pushing sheets of plywood across the saw. Use plain paste wax; skip floor wax, as it contains antislip compounds, and automotive wax, which often contains abrasives. Apply the wax with a steel wool pad and buff it well with a soft rag.

The rails that guide the rip fence will also benefit from a coat of wax. Use a fine steel wool pad as an applicator here, as well. If either the rails or the table are rusty, clean up the spots with some fine sandpaper first, before applying the wax.

■ *looking after blades*

You can spend hours and hours fine-tuning your saw, but if your blades are in bad shape, you're still not going to get a decent cut. In addition, with quality blades costing as much as they do, it really pays to take good care of them. OK, so what constitutes proper care?

There are five things you can do that will keep your blades in good shape as long as possible. I mentioned the first two in the first chapter: Take precautions when tightening and loosening the arbor nut on the saw, and don't set the blades down on the cast iron table. The remaining three are as follows: Keep the blades clean, store them out of harm's way and have them sharpened when they need it.

Sharpening is probably both the easiest and hardest of the three. It is easy because it is not something you can do yourself. Carbide-tipped blades have to be sent to a sharpening shop, which is difficult because you have to find a sharpening shop you can trust with your expensive investment. Ask other woodworkers (especially the professionals) in your area where they have their blades sharpened. Your local hardware store may have a connection with someone who does sharpening. You can also send your blades out of town. Most of the manufacturers are happy to sharpen their products and return them to factory specs. Woodcraft Supply (800-535-4482) in West Virginia also offers an excellent sharpening service.

Regular cleaning helps keep a blade cutting at its best. I keep an aluminum pizza plate hanging in my shop for this purpose. Place the blade in the plate and give it a few squirts of Simple Green household cleaner. Scrub with a brass-bristled wire brush and rinse clean. Dry the blade and wipe it down with some WD-40 to prevent rust and you're back in business.

Once you have a place you can trust, send your blades as soon as they begin to show signs of dulling. These include smoking and burning, excessive splintering and increased feed pressure needed to make a cut. Note: A dirty blade can fool you into thinking it is dull. Pitch and resins, especially from woods such as pine, can build up on the blade and teeth and prevent the blade from cutting as smoothly as it should. Regular cleaning will keep this to a minimum.

Which Cleaner to Use

Any number of recipes for blade cleaners are available, many of which involve nasty chemicals such as paint stripper or lacquer thinner. I, myself, used to be an advocate of oven cleaner. And, sure, they all work, but along with a good portion of the rest of the world, I've begun to look for more environmentally friendly solutions to such tasks. I also learned recently that the lye in oven cleaner actually attacks the binder that holds the carbide together. So I have turned to a relatively "green" method of cleaning my blades. Simple Green is a household cleaner available in the cleaning section of most grocery stores. I use it full strength and it does a great job, and I don't worry about what it is doing to my septic tank. I have also had good results with citrus-oil-based hand cleaner.

Rather than sending your blades to your sharpener loose like carbide-tipped Frisbees, build a transport case for them. Mine is made with 1/4" plywood faces, 3/4" pine sides and is lined with Styrofoam insulation. Cardboard spacers separate the blades so they don't clank against each other.

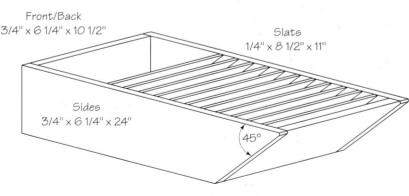

Front/Back
3/4" x 6 1/4" x 10 1/2"

Slats
1/4" x 8 1/2" x 11"

Sides
3/4" x 6 1/4" x 24"

45°

Space slats 3/4" apart.

When they are not in use, store your blades out of harm's way. Storing blades on a nail in the wall is fine as long as the blades don't come in contact with each other. A better solution might be to build a blade rack that holds each blade in its own separate compartment. My rack fits in a drawer under the right-hand extension table.

Making Throat Plates

Most table saws come with two throat plates: One with a somewhat narrow opening for regular blades and one with a wider opening for dado blades. These are adequate for a lot of work, but there are times when you will want to custom-fit the opening in the table to match the blade you are using. One of the most common uses of a custom throat plate is what is called a zero-clearance insert. With a zero-clearance insert, the piece you are cutting has solid support right up to the point where it is being cut. This helps keep tear-out to a minimum. I usually make the blanks for custom throat plates six or so at a time and store them in a drawer until I need them.

[LOOKING AFTER BLADES CONTINUED]

1

I usually make my throat plates from ½" MDF, but any smooth, flat material will do. Cut the material to match the width of the existing plate. Then trace the existing plate onto each blank to lay out the shape of the ends.

2

Cut the blank roughly to shape, then sand it to fit in the opening. The plate should fit snugly in place so it won't rattle around while the saw is in use. You may find it handy to drill a ¾" hole near one end to make it easier to get the plate out of the opening.

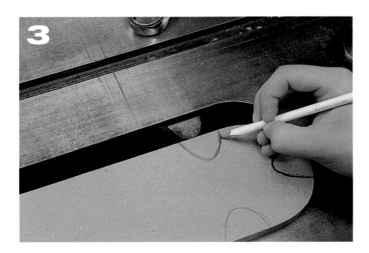

3

Most saws have some sort of flanges in the opening to keep the throat plate from dropping through. I rout out spaces in the underside of the blank for the flanges. This allows the blank to sit below the surface of the saw table. I then add leveling screws so I can adjust the plate until it is dead flush with the table surface. Mark the location of the flanges on the blank to prepare for routing.

Making the Initial Cut

On most saws, the lowest a blade will go is just beneath the surface of the table. This makes cutting the slot in the blank a little tough. Rather than risk dropping the blank onto a spinning blade, I mount one of my dado blades on the saw alone. Since it is only 8" in diameter, there is plenty of clearance above it. I then set the blank in the opening and position the rip fence over it to keep it in place. (Keep the fence to the side so you won't cut it.) Start the saw and raise the blade to cut the opening.

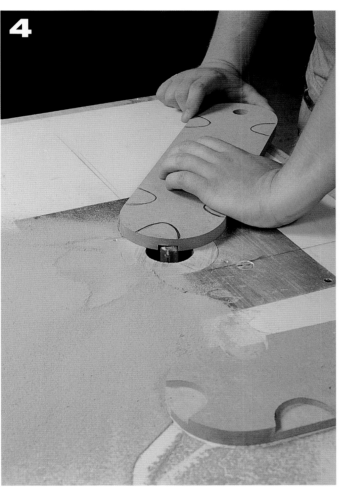

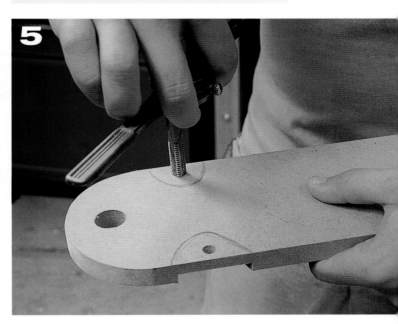

Drill holes in the blank for set screws. I use $3/8$"-16 × $3/8$"-long hex-head set screws. These allow me to adjust the height of the plate from the top side with a hex wrench. MDF taps beautifully with a regular metal-cutting tap (no cutting oil required). Drill the holes with a $5/16$" bit and cut the threads with a $3/8$" tap.

Set up a 1" straight bit in a table-mounted router. Rout away the spaces for the flanges in the underside of the blank. The exact shape of the spaces is not critical. If you don't have access to a router, you can cut the spaces with a sharp chisel.

adding power

Unlike an automobile engine, there is not much you can do to an electric motor to make it more powerful. However, if your saw seems underpowered there are some strategies you can try to squeeze more out of your existing motor. One of these is mainly targeted at contractor's saws, which generally come equipped with a $1\frac{1}{2}$-hp motor that hangs off the back of the saw. The trick here is to upgrade the drive belt and pulleys to a more efficient system. This makes more of the motor's power available at the blade. The other trick is to use a narrow-kerf saw blade. These blades cut a narrower swath through the wood and therefore require less power.

By adding a "hot rod" transmission to your saw, you can eliminate a lot of the vibration and other energy-stealing faults that come with the standard setup. This upgrade consists of two machined steel pulleys, which run much truer than the stock pulleys, and a link belt, which performs much better than a standard V-belt.

Blade Stabilizers

When you use a thin-kerf blade, the thinner saw body is more prone to vibration, which can make for rougher cuts. A partial solution is to use a blade stabilizer. A stabilizer is a big washer that is installed between the blade and the standard cup washer that comes with the saw. This extra piece of metal adds support to the blade and helps cut down on vibration. The only compromise is that it reduces the maximum cut the blade can make – a small trade-off for increased performance.

Actually, the folks at Forrest recommend that you use a stabilizer with all blades, both thin and regular kerf. This is not because Forrest blades need a stabilizer, but rather that the extra support a stabilizer offers can't hurt anything, and probably helps out in many situations.

The difference isn't a lot – a kerf of $1/8$" for the standard blade versus $3/32$" for the thin-kerf blade – but that $1/32$" adds up to approximately a 25-percent gain in power.

wall-hung spice cabinet

A FINE ADDITION TO A KITCHEN, OR any place you need storage for small items, this wall-hung cabinet offers a lot of table saw technique in a small package. Dadoes, rabbets, slip joints, even cove-cutting, it's all there. In fact, the design incorporates so many different techniques, it is the project I use when teaching my Table Saw Trickery weekend workshop. This is the reason I can say, with confidence, you can easily build this cabinet in a couple of days.

The style of the cabinet is early American — the sort of cabinet a country furniture maker would build for his local clientele to store spices in. The case is joined with dadoes and rabbets with reproduction cut nails lending reinforcement and something of a rustic feel. The door uses traditional raised-panel construction. The bevels on the panel were created with a cove cut, and the corners of the frame are joined with slip joints. With the exception of the hole in the door for the knob, and the screw holes for the hinges, the entire cabinet is built with the table saw. So, in addition to completing a good-looking project, you can really ramp up your table saw skills in the process. The entire cabinet can be built from a single 1×8×10 (or a 1×6×10 if you are lucky and the board has very few knots).

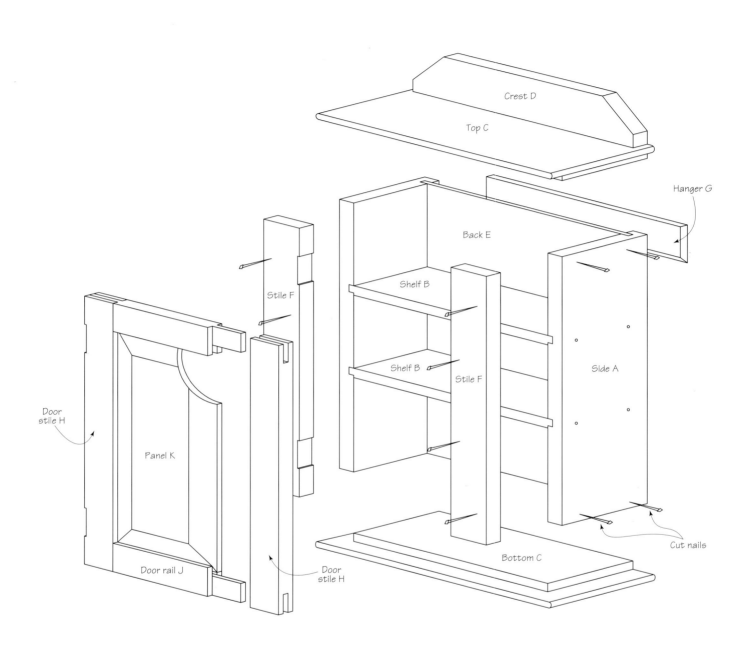

Crest D

Top C

Hanger G

Back E

Stile F

Shelf B

Shelf B

Stile F

Side A

Door
stile H

Panel K

Door rail J

Door
stile H

Bottom C

Cut nails

MATERIALS LIST inches

REFERENCE	QUANTITY	PART	STOCK	THICKNESS	WIDTH	LENGTH
A	2	sides	pine 1×6	$3/4$	$4^1/_2$	$14^1/_4$
B	2	shelves	pine 1×6	$1/2$	$3^7/_8$	$10^3/_4$
C	2	top/bottom	pine 1×6	$3/4$	$5^1/_2$	$12^3/_8$
D	1	crest	pine 1×6	$3/4$	$2^1/_4$	$11^3/_4$
E	1	back	plywood	$1/4$	$10^3/_4$	$13^7/_8$
F	2	case stiles	pine 1×6	$3/4$	$1^7/_8$	$14^1/_4$
G	2	hangers	pine 1×6	$3/8$	2	$10^1/_4$

door

REFERENCE	QUANTITY	PART	STOCK	THICKNESS	WIDTH	LENGTH
H	2	stiles	pine 1×6	$3/4$	$1^1/_2$	$14^1/_4$
J	2	rails	pine 1×6	$3/4$	$1^1/_2$	8
K	1	panel	pine 1×6	$3/4$	$5^1/_2$	$11^3/_4$

HARDWARE

24 cut nails $1^1/_2$" long — Rockler #32288

2 hinges $1^1/_2$"-long × $1^1/_4$"-wide — Rockler #25759

1 knob 1" diameter — Rockler #61647

Rockler Woodworking and Hardware, 800-279-4441, www.rockler.com

MATERIALS LIST millimeters

REFERENCE	QUANTITY	PART	STOCK	THICKNESS	WIDTH	LENGTH
A	2	sides	pine 1×6	19	115	362
B	2	shelves	pine 1×6	13	98	273
C	2	top/bottom	pine 1×6	19	140	315
D	1	crest	pine 1×6	19	57	298
E	1	back	plywood	6	273	352
F	2	case stiles	pine 1×6	19	47	362
G	2	hangers	pine 1×6	10	51	260

door

REFERENCE	QUANTITY	PART	STOCK	THICKNESS	WIDTH	LENGTH
H	2	stiles	pine 1×6	19	38	362
J	2	rails	pine 1×6	19	38	203
K	1	panel	pine 1×6	19	140	298

HARDWARE

24 cut nails 38mm long — Rockler #32288

2 hinges 38mm-long × 32mm-wide — Rockler #25759

1 knob 25mm diameter — Rockler #61647

Rockler Woodworking and Hardware, 800-279-4441, www.rockler.com

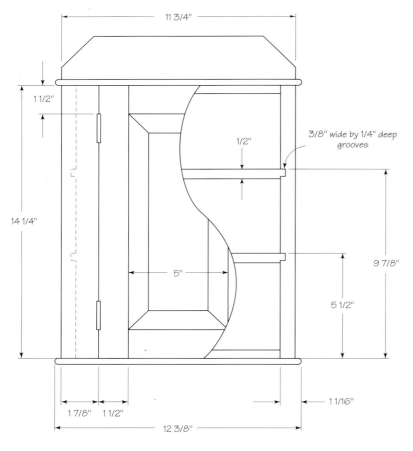

Front View

11 3/4"

1 1/2"

14 1/4"

1/2"

3/8" wide by 1/4" deep grooves

5"

9 7/8"

5 1/2"

1 7/8" 1 1/2"

1 1/16"

12 3/8"

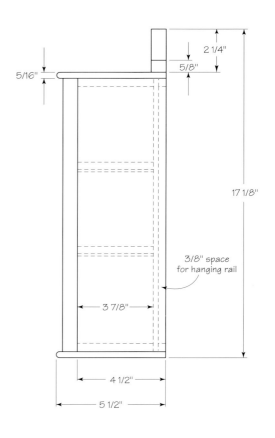

Side View

5/16"

2 1/4"

5/8"

17 1/8"

3/8" space for hanging rail

3 7/8"

4 1/2"

5 1/2"

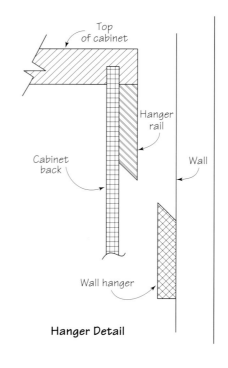

Top of cabinet

Hanger rail

Cabinet back

Wall

Wall hanger

Hanger Detail

Cut the sides, shelves, top and bottom to size. Resaw the shelves to the specified thickness in two passes.

Cut ³⁄₈"-wide by ¼"-deep grooves across the sides as shown in the front view. Attach a stop-block to an auxiliary fence on the miter gauge to keep the spacing of the grooves consistent. See "Cutting Dadoes and Grooves" in chapter two, "Joinery."

Without changing the height of the dado head, set up a rabbeting fence and rabbet the ends of the shelves to fit snugly in the grooves cut in the sides. See "Cutting Rabbets" in chapter two, "Joinery."

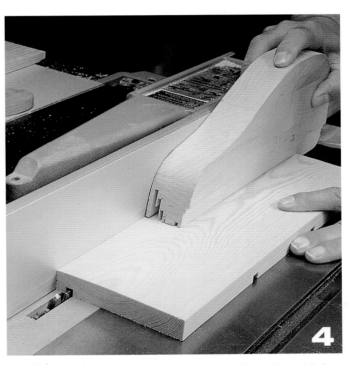

Cut a ¼"-wide by ¼"-deep groove in the sides, top and bottom to contain the back. The groove should be ³⁄₈" in from the back edge of the pieces.

Sand the shelves and the sides. Spread glue in the grooves and insert the shelves, rabbet side up. Nail through the sides to reinforce the joints. The back edges of the shelves should be flush with the outer side of the back groove. If you are using cut nails, put a scrap down on your bench so the nail heads in the first side (which may protrude slightly) do not mar your benchtop when you nail the second side.

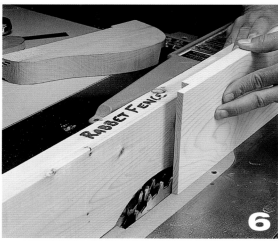

Increase the width of the dado head, and reinstall the rabbeting fence. Rabbet the front edge and both ends of the top and bottom. The rabbets should be $7/16''$ deep and about $1\,1/16''$ wide. Adjust the width (determined by the height of the blade) so the distance from shoulder to shoulder matches the distance between the sides of the partially assembled case.

Round over the thin edges of the top and bottom with a block plane and sandpaper. Be careful planing the ends. If you cut all the way across, the edge is likely to chip. To avoid this, plane almost all the way across then turn around and plane the last bit in the opposite direction. Sand the top and bottom.

Cut the crest rail to size. Turn the miter gauge to a 45° angle and cut the corners off the crest rail. Use a stop-block to keep the cuts consistent. Sand the crest rail, then glue it to the top, flush with the back edge. Cut the back to size and slide it in place. Glue and nail the top and bottom to the side/shelf assembly.

Cut the case stiles to size. Set up a $3/4''$-wide dado blade and cut the mortises for the hinges across the edge of one of the stiles. The mortises should be about $1/16''$ deep. Use two stop-blocks to control their width. Cut one mortise, then turn the piece end over end to cut the second.

10

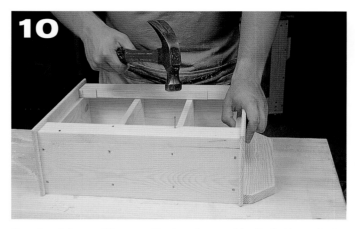

Plane the shelves and the case sides to make everything flush. Glue and nail the case stiles to the front of the cabinet. Cut the hangers to size and rip one edge at a 45° angle. Glue one of the hangers to the back of the cabinet as shown in the Hanger Detail earlier in this chapter. The other hanger is attached to the wall.

11

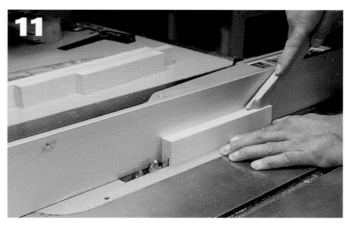

Cut the door stiles and rails to size. Cut a ¼" groove centered on one edge of each piece for the panel.

12

Cut slip joints to join the corners of the door frame. Base the spacing of the joint on the panel groove. The tenons should be cut on the rails. When cutting the mortises in the ends of the stiles, the height of the blade should be about 1". This accommodates the groove cut in the rails, which shows up as a narrower tenon. See "Cutting Slip Joints" in chapter two, "Joinery."

13

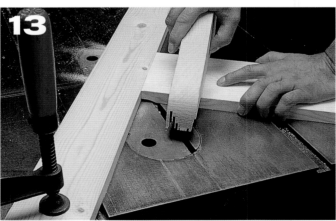

Set up a piece of scrap wood at an angle across your saw as a fence. The fence should cross over the blade because you are cutting half a cove. See "Cutting Half a Cove" in chapter three, "Shaping." Make the cut in small bites.

14

Sand and assemble the door. Mortise one side of the door for the hinges as you did for the cabinet stile. When you have the saw set up, cut the mortise in a piece of scrap first, to check the depth. After you cut the mortises, install the hinges. Use only one screw in each leaf until you are happy with the fit. Finish the cabinet to suit.

tabletop valet

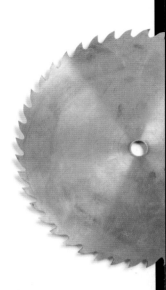

FEW PEOPLE WOULDN'T FIND THIS valet a handy companion. Place it on your dresser as a convenient cache for your wallet and keys when you come home from work. Or place it near the front door where the drawers can hold stamps, money for the paper carrier and a water pistol for scaring away the errant raffle ticket salesperson. Either way, you can use the mirror for a last-minute check before heading out to face the world.

From a technical standpoint, the case and mirror frame present a tour de force of mitered construction. The drawers are constructed using lock joints and dadoes, and the mirror frame itself offers a chance to see how you can create some classy mouldings using a standard saw blade. In all, the valet makes good use of the table saw's many strengths, while the end result is well worth the effort.

MATERIALS LIST inches

REFERENCE	QUANTITY	PART	STOCK	THICKNESS	WIDTH	LENGTH	COMMENTS
A	2	top/bottom	walnut	$9/16$	$7^3/4$	$17^1/4$	
B	2	sides	walnut	$9/16$	$7^3/4$	$3^3/4$	
C	1	divider	walnut	$9/16$	$7^1/4$	$2^7/8$	cut to fit
D	1	back	walnut	$3/8$	3	$16^1/2$	
E	2	feet	walnut	$7/8$	$1^1/8$	$9^1/4$	
F	2	uprights	walnut	$9/16$	3	$10^1/2$	
G	1	crest rail	walnut	1	2	$10^1/2$	
H	2	stiles	walnut	1	$1^1/4$	$14^1/8$	
J	1	rail	walnut	1	$1^1/4$	$10^1/2$	
K	2	drawer fronts	walnut	$3/4$	$2^5/8$	$7^3/4$	
L	4	drawer sides	walnut	$1/2$	$2^5/8$	$6^3/4$	
M	2	drawer backs	walnut	$1/2$	2	$7^1/4$	
N	2	drawer bottoms	walnut	$1/4$	6	$7^1/4$	
P	2	pulls	walnut	$5/8$	$5/8$	$2^1/8$	
Q	2	retaining strips	walnut	$3/8$	$5/8$	$9^1/2$	
R	2	retaining strips	walnut	$3/8$	$5/8$	$13^1/8$	

HARDWARE

Mirror	$8^3/4" \times 12^1/4"$	
Steel studs	$5/16"$ diameter $\times 3/4"$	
4 screws	No. $8 \times 2"$	To attach uprights
4 screws	No. $8 \times 1^1/4"$	To attach feet
8 brass screws	No. $8 \times 1/2"$	To attach retaining strips
2 screws	No. $6 \times 1^1/4"$	To attach pulls

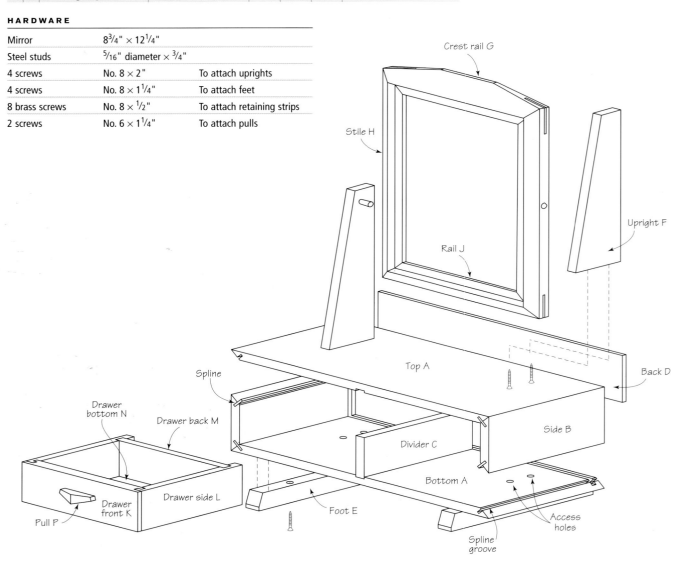

Crest rail G

Stile H

Rail J

Upright F

Top A

Spline

Back D

Drawer bottom N

Drawer back M

Side B

Divider C

Drawer side L

Bottom A

Pull P

Drawer front K

Foot E

Spline groove

Access holes

REFERENCE	QUANTITY	PART	STOCK	THICKNESS	WIDTH	LENGTH	COMMENTS
A	2	top/bottom	walnut	14	197	438	
B	2	sides	walnut	14	197	95	
C	1	divider	walnut	14	184	73	cut to fit
D	1	back	walnut	10	76	419	
E	2	feet	walnut	22	29	235	
F	2	uprights	walnut	14	76	267	
G	1	crest rail	walnut	25	51	267	
H	2	stiles	walnut	25	32	359	
J	1	rail	walnut	25	38	267	
K	2	drawer fronts	walnut	19	67	197	
L	4	drawer sides	walnut	13	67	171	
M	2	drawer backs	walnut	13	51	184	
N	2	drawer bottoms	walnut	6	152	184	
P	2	pulls	walnut	16	16	54	
Q	2	retaining strips	walnut	10	16	242	
R	2	retaining strips	walnut	10	16	333	

HARDWARE

Mirror	222mm × 311mm	
Steel studs	8mm diameter × 19mm	
4 screws	No. 8 × 51mm	To attach uprights
4 screws	No. 8 × 32mm	To attach feet
8 brass screws	No. 8 × 13mm	To attach retaining strips
2 screws	No. 6 × 32mm	To attach pulls

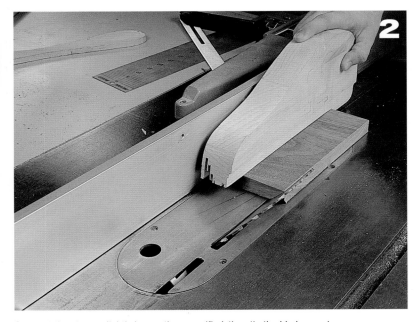

Cut the top, bottom, sides and divider from a single board. Plane the board to thickness and cut it to the specified width. Then lay out the crosscuts, labeling the adjoining ends. This way, after you cut the miters you can assemble the case so the grain continues from piece to piece on three of the four corners.

Crosscut the pieces slightly longer than specified, then tip the blade over to 45° and miter the ends. Use a stop-block and an extension fence on the miter gauge to make sure the top and bottom end up the same length. Run the sides, however, along the fence. They are much wider than they are long, so running along the fence is actually safer and more precise than using the miter gauge in this situation. See "Cutting Miter Joints" in chapter two, "Joinery."

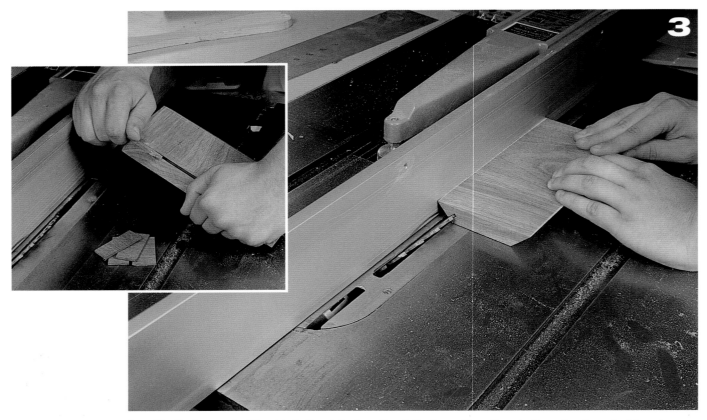

Reposition the fence and cut the slots for the reinforcing splines in the faces of the miter cuts. Remember, the grain of the splines should run across the joint for added strength, so it is easier to make the spline in relatively narrow pieces and use several pieces in each joint. Be sure to use a push stick and a zero-clearance throat plate when cutting the splines.

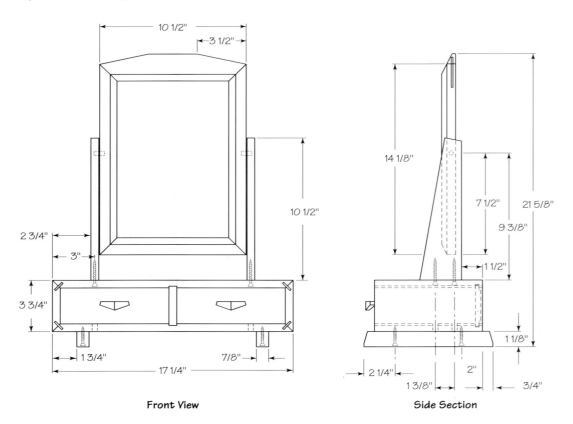

Front View   Side Section

Cut a groove for the back in both sides, the top and the bottom. Measure the length of the grooves, and cut the back slightly smaller than the maximum size the grooves would allow. Rabbet the edges of the back to fit in the grooves. Also cut a shallow groove across the top and bottom, centered for the divider. See "Cutting Dadoes and Grooves" in chapter two, "Joinery."

For the best possible clamping pressure, cut angled glue blocks and glue them right to the sides, top and bottom. No need to go overboard with the glue; a thin bead will provide enough holding power without causing too big a headache when it comes time to cut off the glue block.

Assemble the case without glue first, to make sure everything fits. You'll have to spring the case a little to get the last corner into place. When you are happy with the fit, disassemble and apply glue to the miters and the splines, then clamp the joints firmly together. Take a quick measurement and cut the divider to fit. Glue it in its grooves.

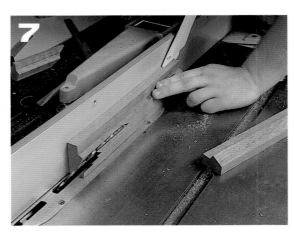

Cut the pieces for the mirror frame to the profile shown in the Moulding Details at right. You'll have to reposition the rip fence when you make the second angled cut on the crest rail, as it is wider than the rest of the pieces.

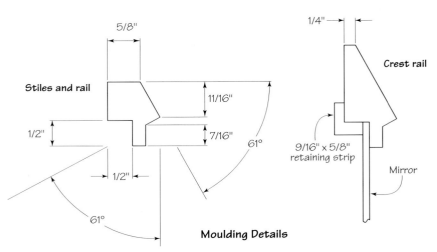

Stiles and rail

5/8"
11/16"
1/2"
7/16"
1/2"
61°
61°

1/4"
Crest rail
9/16" x 5/8" retaining strip
Mirror

Moulding Details

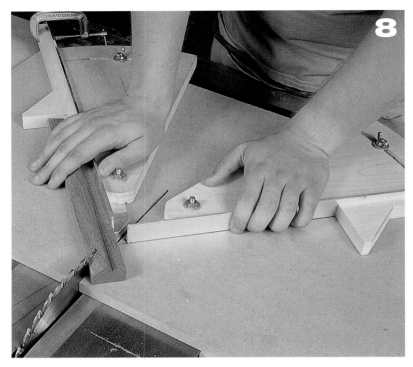

Miter the corners of the frame, using a stop-block to control the lengths of the pieces. Glue up the frame again, using angled glue blocks to apply pressure directly across the joints. I know this requires extra work, but the results are worth it. Also make the taper cuts on the top edge of the crest rail.

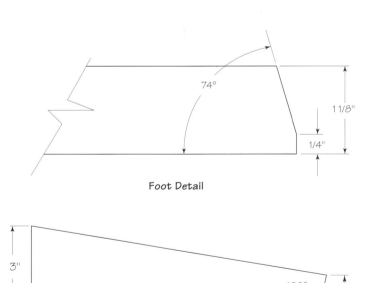

74°

1 1/8"

1/4"

Foot Detail

3"

102°

1 3/16"

10 1/2"

Upright Detail

When the glue is dry, carefully place the frame in a cradle and cut slots for reinforcing splines. Cut the splines to fit in the slots and glue in place. Trim and sand the splines flush with the frame.

Bevel the ends of the feet as shown in the Foot Detail at left. Use an extension fence on the miter gauge and a stop-block to make the cuts consistent. Drill oversize holes in the feet and screw them to the underside of the case.

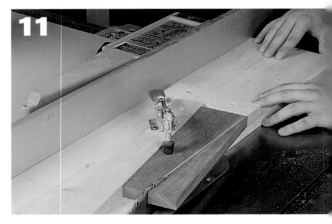

Set up the stop-blocks on the carrier board and taper the uprights. Drill holes in the case for the screws used to attach the uprights. You also need to drill access holes in the bottom so you can get a screwdriver through to tighten the screws. See "Cutting Tapers" in chapter three, "Shaping."

12

Drill the sides of the frame and the uprights for the steel studs that suspend the frame. Lay out the centers of these holes carefully; any error and the mirror will be crooked. Screw the uprights to the case and pop the frame into place.

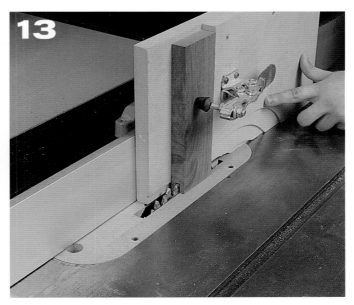

13

Cut the drawer parts to size and check to make sure they fit in the drawer openings. Cut lock joints to join the sides of the drawers to the drawer front, and a simple groove in the sides to catch the drawer back. Also cut grooves in the sides and front for the bottom. Assemble the drawers and reinforce the joints with small finish nails. See "Making a Lock Joint" in chapter two, "Joinery."

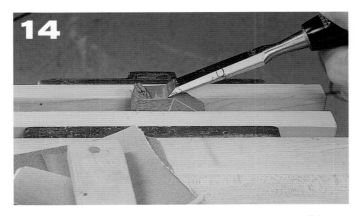

14

You can crosscut the drawer pulls to length on the table saw, but you'll have to make the various taper cuts by hand; the pieces are just too small to taper safely on the saw. Once the drawers fit properly, glue drawer stops in the openings to keep the drawers from sliding too far into the case.

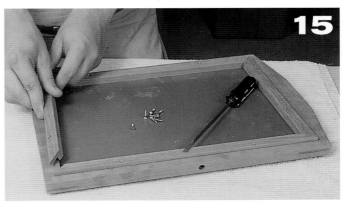

15

As a final step, set the mirror in the frame and hold it in place with retaining strips. The strips are screwed in place so you can replace the mirror relatively easily if necessary. Finish the valet as desired.

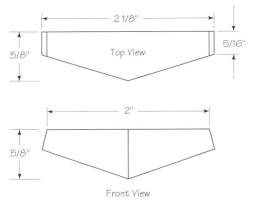

2 1/8"

Top View

5/8"

5/16"

2"

5/8"

Front View

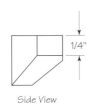

1/4"

Side View

demilune table

DEMILUNE TABLES FALL UNDER THE general category of occasional tables. This category also includes sofa tables, coffee tables, end tables and the like. The relatively small dimensions of the table shown here make it suitable for any number of different rooms. In an entryway it could provide a handy surface for sorting the daily mail or as a repository for car keys. In the dining room it functions as a serving table or a display surface for the family portrait gallery. In a bedroom it could be used as a dressing table.

Or consider scaling up the size of the table for a different use. My grandmother had a pair of demilune tables that worked in conjunction with her big drop-leaf dining table. With the leaves down, the two half-rounds sat next to the main table, making a nicely sized table for six. With the leaves up on the main table, and the half-round tables at either end, a dozen people could sit down comfortably, and

fourteen or more could sit if you didn't mind being cozy. The half-rounds could also be placed against the wall as serving tables. It was a versatile setup.

As a woodworking project, the table packs some exciting techniques into an elegant package. The biggest challenge is in making the curved aprons and then cutting the joinery in the bent pieces. The pieces are shaped over a form using a technique known as bentwood lamination. This involves cutting a piece of wood into thin, flexible strips and then gluing the strips over a curved form. When the glue dries, the resulting lamination will hold the shape of the form. Once you have the curved pieces, you'll need to make some shaped blocks to help hold them in the proper orientation as you cut them to length and then cut the tenons on their ends. In all, this project will put you and your saw to the test.

[PROJECT THREE]

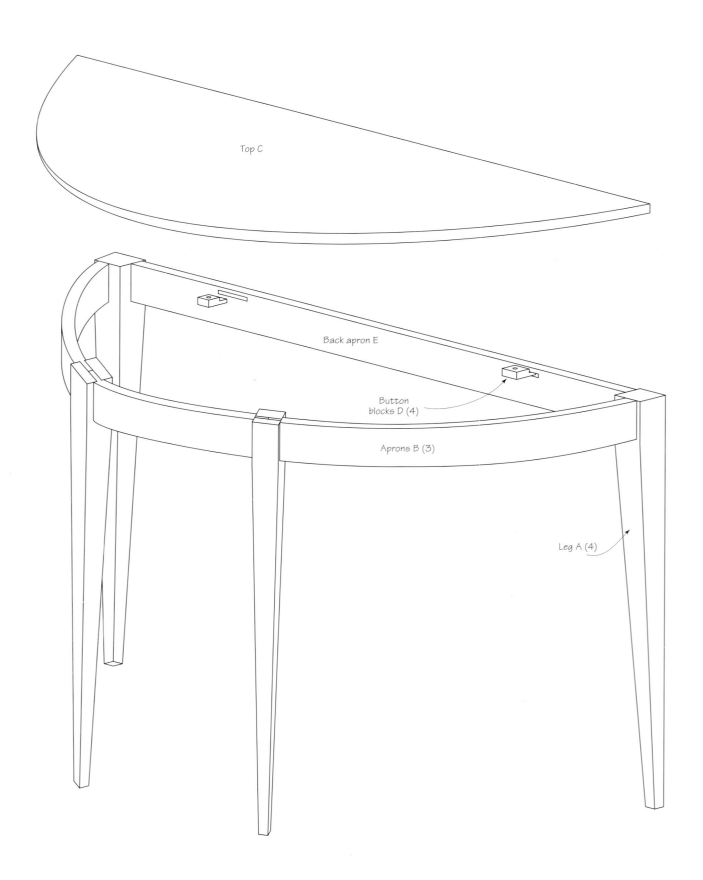

Top C

Back apron E

Button
blocks D (4)

Aprons B (3)

Leg A (4)

MATERIALS LIST inches

REFERENCE	QUANTITY	PART	STOCK	THICKNESS	WIDTH	LENGTH	COMMENTS
A	4	legs	cherry	$1^3/4$	$1^3/4$	$27^1/4$	
B	3	aprons	cherry	$3/4$	$2^5/8$	21	each made from 6 strips — $1/8" \times 3" \times 24"$
C	1	top	cherry	$3/4$	$18^7/8$	$40^1/8$	
D	4	button blocks	cherry	$3/4$	1	$1^1/2$	
E	1	back apron	cherry	$3/4$	$2^5/8$	$35^1/2$	

MATERIALS LIST millimeters

REFERENCE	QUANTITY	PART	STOCK	THICKNESS	WIDTH	LENGTH	COMMENTS
A	4	legs	cherry	45	45	692	
B	3	aprons	cherry	19	67	533	each made from 6 strips — 3mm × 76mm × 610mm
C	1	top	cherry	19	479	1019	
D	4	button blocks	cherry	19	25	38	
E	1	back apron	cherry	19	67	902	

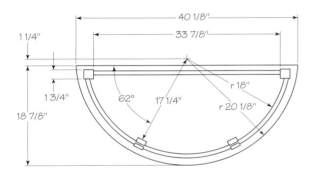

Leg taper starts 3" down from the top.
Back legs taper on two sides.
Front legs taper on three sides.

Mortise Detail

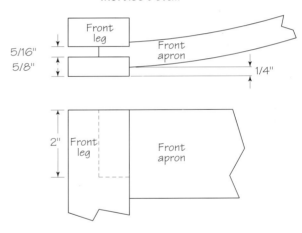

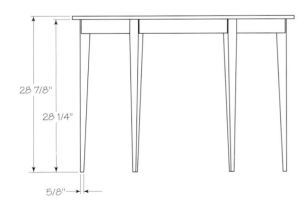

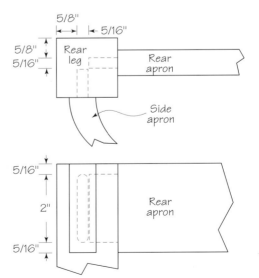

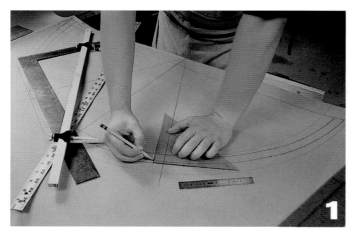

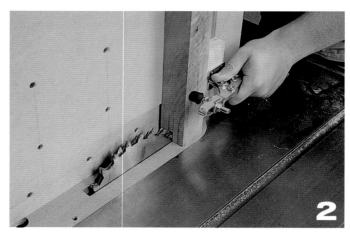

Make a full-size drawing of the table, showing the exact curve of the aprons and the placement of the legs. The two front legs should be tangent to the curve of the apron as shown on the previous page. Having a full-size drawing is invaluable when working with curves and other pieces involving angles that are not square, as you can check your work right on the layout.

Cut the legs to the size given in the materials list. Cut the mortises in the legs before making the taper cuts. The mortises in the two front legs are simple slots. Cut them with a dado head on the table saw. Set the dado for a $5/16$" cut. Make the blade height 2". Clamp the legs vertically in the tenoning jig and adjust the jig laterally to position the slot as shown in the Mortise Detail earlier in this chapter.

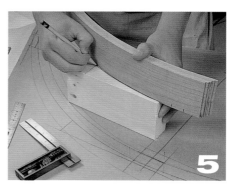

Cut the mortises in the back legs with a plunge router. Clamp the legs side by side as shown, and use an edge guide to control the position of the bit. The second leg provides extra support for the router as the mortises are near the end of the leg. Clamp blocks of wood to the top of the legs to serve as stops to control the length of the mortises. The mortise dimensions are shown in the Rear Leg Joinery Details on the previous page.

Once the joinery is cut, you can taper the legs, using the same setup for both cuts. The back legs are tapered on their two inside faces; the front legs are tapered on three faces. The innermost face can be cut with the same setup you used for the rear legs. The second face requires a different setup, as the taper is shallower. The third face requires yet another setup because it uses the second face (which you just cut) as a reference. See "Cutting Tapers" in chapter three, "Shaping."

After you have bent the aprons (see "Bentwood Lamination" later in this chapter), you'll need to make two curved blocks — one for the front leg/apron joinery and one for the back — to hold them in the proper orientation as you cut them to length. Make the blocks from a straight piece of 2×4. Lay out the blocks on your full-size drawing. Trace one of the aprons to get the curve right, then make the cuts with a band saw.

Position each apron piece on the full-size drawing to mark its length. Mark both the overall length (including the tenons) and the shoulders where the apron meets the legs.

Cut a spacer block so its width matches the length of the tenon. Use this spacer to hold the curved block the proper distance above the saw table as you screw the curved block to the tenoning jig. Start with the block for the front leg/apron joinery.

Hold the curved block against the miter gauge and cradle the apron in it to make the cut. Align the shoulder mark on the apron with the end of the block, then slide both pieces along the miter gauge to position the apron in relation to the blade.

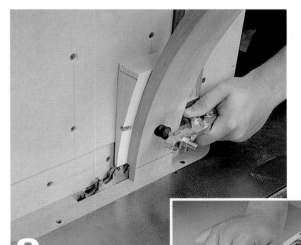

Mark the tenon positions on the aprons according to the layout on the full-size drawing. Clamp the apron against the curved block with its end on the table. Set up a $\frac{3}{8}$"-wide dado and adjust its height to match the tenon length. Position the jig laterally to cut the outside tenon face (the one closest to the jig) first. After making this cut for each tenon, reposition the jig to make the second cut. Start with the tenon being too fat, then add shims between the fences to adjust the jig until the tenon fits snugly in its mortise. Repeat the process for the back leg/apron joints.

After you cut the tenons on the saw, you'll need to trim them to fit in the mortises. Once everything fits, assemble the table and clamp it together without glue to make sure everything pulls up tight. I used a pipe clamp across the back apron, two band clamps around the entire table, and two small clamps on the front legs to squeeze the mortises together. When you are satisfied with the fit, disassemble and sand all the pieces. Apply glue, and reclamp.

Edge-glue pieces to make a panel wide enough for the top. Cut the top to the proper shape and sand it well. Place the top upside down on your bench on top of an old towel (for protection). Center the base on the top and join the two together with button blocks. Cut the slots for the blocks with a wing cutter mounted in your router.

bentwood lamination

There are essentially three ways to come up with a curved piece of wood. One, you could saw the piece out of solid stock. This works for shallow bends but generally means you have to start out with a really thick piece of wood. If the bend is fairly sharp, the sawn piece may be weak because parts of it will contain short grain. Two, you can steam solid pieces. This works quite well but requires you to have a steamer. Three, you can glue together a series of thin, flexible strips over a curved form, a process known as bentwood or strip lamination. The technique yields pieces that are strong and is easily accomplished with common shop equipment.

The first step is to build a form. I generally build up forms from MDF. Make the form at least as wide as the pieces you'll be bending. If the curve you are after is a true arc (part of a circle), you can lay it out using a compass (or a set of trammel points). If the curve is not part of a circle, you have to be a little more creative. A flexible drawing spline (the curved, silver thing in the photo) may help you draw a smooth curve.

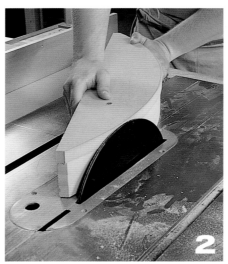

Cut the form pieces roughly to shape, then screw them together in a stack and sand them to match the actual curve. Make the form (and the actual lamination) several inches longer than the finished dimension of the piece you need. The ends of a lamination often aren't bent as accurately as the middle part. If the piece is longer than needed, you can cut away the part that isn't as good.

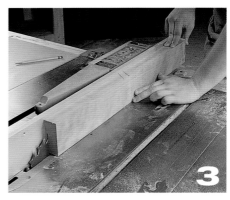

Rip the laminations to thickness. For laminations over 2" wide, I make the cut in two passes as shown. Again, make the pieces several inches longer than you need, the final inch or two may be spoiled as it passes the blade. Cut the pieces at least ¼" wider than the finished dimension you're after. To find what thickness works well, cut some test pieces and bend them over your form.

Apply glue to one side of each lamination and stack the pieces up. I find a printer's brayer does a great job of spreading an even coat of glue. For most bends, yellow wood glue will work well. However, for particularly severe bends, or those such as rocking chair rockers that will be subjected to a lot of stress, use an adhesive that forms a more rigid bond, such as plastic resin glue.

Once the glue is spread, clamp the bend over the form. Try to keep the laminations from slipping from one side to the other — not an easy trick when everything is slippery with glue. You'll need a lot of clamps. Adding a couple of extra pieces (without glue) to the stack will help spread the clamping pressure, reducing the need for a few clamps.

When the glue has dried (leave each bend you make in the form a minimum of 24 hours), take off the clamps, then scrape away the squeeze-out with a cabinet scraper (dried glue is hard on jointer knives). Trim the edge straight on the jointer. Be sure to hold the piece tight to the fence to keep the edge square. If you don't have a jointer, straighten the edge as well as possible with a hand plane.

Cut the piece to width on the table saw. Start with the leading edge on the table and the rest curling up in the air. Carefully push the piece past the blade, rolling it to keep the part being cut in contact with the table.

suppliers

BIESEMEYER MANUFACTURING
216 South Alma School Road, Suite 3
Mesa, Arizona 85210
800-782-1831
www.biesemeyer.com
Fences, guards, splitters

CMT USA, INC
307-F Pomona Drive
Greensboro, North Carolina 27407
888-268-2487
www.cmtusa.com
Cove cutter, carbide-tipped tooling

FORREST MANUFACTURING
461 River Road
Clifton, New Jersey 07014
800-733-7111
forrest.woodmall.com
Carbide-tipped saw blades, dado sets, sharpening

FREUD TOOLS
218 Feld Avenue
High Point, North Carolina 27263
800-334-4107
www.freudtools.com
Carbide-tipped saw blades, dado sets, tooling

LRH ENTERPRISES
9250 Independence Avenue
Chatsworth, California 91311
800-423-2544
www.lrhent.com
Magic Molder

WINDY RIDGE WOODWORKS
6751 Hollenbach Rd.
New Tripoli, PA 18066
610 767-4515
Fine furniture and woodworking instruction

WOODCRAFT
P.O. Box 1686
Parkersburg, West Virginia 26102-1686
800-225-1153
www.woodcraft.com
Woodworking hardware and accessories

index